The Experiences of Black and Minority Ethnic Academics

Recent research suggests that Black and minority ethnic (BME) academics remain underrepresented, particularly at senior levels in higher education, and tend to be concentrated in new, post-1992 universities. This book provides an original comparative study of BME academics in both the UK and the USA, two different yet similar cultural and political climates, considering issues of inequality, difference and identity in the academy.

Presenting a distinctive and engaging voice, the book discusses the complexity of race, gender and identity in the context of higher education, an area that continues to appear to be dominated by White, middle-class values and perspectives. Chapters offer an up-to-date commentary on the purpose, failures and potential of research on race, gender and identity, and its place within contemporary education and sociology. The book broadens the understanding of educational research, considering both sociological and cultural discourse, as well as examining racialised and gendered identities from a theoretical and analytical standpoint. The book closes by offering suggestions for viable policy shifts in this area.

The Experiences of Black and Minority Ethnic Academics will be of key interest to researchers, academics and postgraduate students in the field of education, as well as sociologists wanting to learn more about Black and minority academics in higher education.

Kalwant Bhopal is Reader in Education at the University of Southampton, UK.

Routledge Research in Higher Education

Integrative Learning
International research and practice
Edited by Daniel Blackshields, James Cronin, Bettie Higgs, Shane Kilcommins, Marian McCarthy and Anthony Ryan

Developing Creativities in Higher Music Education
International perspectives and practices
Edited by Pamela Burnard

Academic Governance
Disciplines and policy
Jenny M. Lewis

Refocusing the Self in Higher Education
A phenomenological perspective
Glen L. Sherman

Activity Theory, Authentic Learning and Emerging Technologies
Towards a transformative higher education pedagogy
Edited by Vivienne Bozalek, Dick Ng'ambi, Denise Wood, Jan Herrington, Joanne Hardman and Alan Amory

Understanding HIV and STI Prevention for College Students
Edited by Leo Wilton, Robert T. Palmer and Dina C. Maramba

From Vocational to Professional Education
Educating for social welfare
Jens-Christian Smeby and Molly Sutphen

Academic Building in Net-based Higher Education
Moving beyond learning
Edited by Trine Fossland, Helle Mathiasen and Mariann Solberg

University Access and Success
Capabilities, diversity and social justice
Merridy Wilson-Strydom

Reconsidering English Studies in Indian Higher Education
Suman Gupta, Richard Allen, Subarno Chattarji and Supriya Chaudhuri

Globally Networked Teaching in the Humanities
Theories and practices
Edited by Alexandra Schultheis Moore and Sunka Simon

Higher Education Access and Choice for Latino Students
Critical findings and theoretical perspectives
Edited by Patricia A. Pérez and Miguel Ceja

The Experiences of Black and Minority Ethnic Academics
A comparative study of the unequal academy
Kalwant Bhopal

The Experiences of Black and Minority Ethnic Academics

A comparative study of the unequal academy

Kalwant Bhopal

Routledge
Taylor & Francis Group
LONDON AND NEW YORK

First published 2016 by Routledge

2 Park Square, Milton Park, Abingdon, Oxfordshire OX14 4RN
711 Third Avenue, New York, NY 10017

Routledge is an imprint of the Taylor & Francis Group, an informa business

First issued in paperback 2017

Copyright © 2016 K. Bhopal

The right of K. Bhopal to be identified as author of this work has been asserted by her in accordance with sections 77 and 78 of the Copyright, Designs and Patents Act 1988.

All rights reserved. No part of this book may be reprinted or reproduced or utilised in any form or by any electronic, mechanical, or other means, now known or hereafter invented, including photocopying and recording, or in any information storage or retrieval system, without permission in writing from the publishers.

Notice:
Product or corporate names may be trademarks or registered trademarks, and are used only for identification and explanation without intent to infringe.

British Library Cataloguing in Publication Data
A catalogue record for this book is available from the British Library

Library of Congress Cataloging in Publication Data
Bhopal, Kalwant.
The experiences of black and minority ethnic academics : a comparative study of the unequal academy / Kalwant Bhopal.
pages cm
Includes bibliographical references and index.
1. Faculty integration—Great Britain. 2. Faculty integration—United States. 3. Minorities in higher education—Great Britain. 4. Minorities in higher education—United States. 5. Minority college teachers—Great Britain. 6. Minority college teachers—United States. 7. College teachers, Black—Great Britain. 8. African American college teachers. I. Title.
Lb2332.6.B56 2015
378.1'982—dc23
2014049578

ISBN: 978-0-415-73669-5 (hbk)
ISBN: 978-0-8153-5699-8 (pbk)

Typeset in Baskerville
by Swales & Willis Ltd, Exeter, Devon, UK

To all the 'outsiders' who struggle to find a place in the academy

Contents

	List of figures and tables	x
	Acknowledgements	xi
1	Introduction	1
2	Higher education in the UK and USA	7
3	The research and methodology	43
4	Theoretical understandings of identity in the academy	61
5	'Outsiders' in the academy?	86
6	Climbing the ladder: promotion and progression	113
7	Inclusion, equality and social justice	129
8	Conclusions	154
	Index	158

Figures and tables

Figures

2.1	Full-time faculty in postsecondary institutions by academic rank, race/ethnicity and sex (USA)	32

Tables

2.1	Academic staff by academic employment function 2012/13	13
2.2	All staff by full-time academic employment, occupational classification and sex 2012/13	14
2.3	Academic staff by ethnic minority group 2012/13	15
2.4	Academic staff at senior management by ethnicity 2012/13	15
2.5	Academic professors by ethnicity 2012/13	15
2.6	Academic professors by gender 2012/13	16
2.7	Percentage of first year UK ethnic minority students in higher education 2012/13	18
2.8	Number of degrees conferred by race/ethnicity (USA)	30
3.1	Gender and employment level of respondents (UK)	44
3.2	Ethnic background of respondents (UK)	45
3.3	Gender and employment level of respondents (USA)	45

Acknowledgements

I would like to thank the participants for their time and willingness to participate in the research and for sharing their stories with me. I would like to thank Michelle Harricharan for conducting a number of the interviews and analysing some of the data. I am hugely indebted to Hazel Brown for reading earlier drafts of the chapters and providing useful comments. During 2011, I spent my sabbatical at the University of Wisconsin-Madison and I am grateful for the support I received (and continue to receive) from Carl Grant, Gloria Ladson-Billings and Michael Apple. It was during that time that the ideas for this book were first discussed. Thank you to my wonderful children, Sachin, Deva, Yasmin and Dylan, and my co-pilot Martin for their continued support.

1 Introduction

The international global economic crises have led to significant insecurities in the labour market, both on a national and international level. Economic recession has affected European countries such as Greece, Italy and Spain. In the UK, changes in Coalition government policy making between 2010 and 2015 saw huge spending cuts in education and it is those who remain marginalised and disadvantaged who have been most affected. Alan Milburn's report (2012) on social mobility outlines significant inequalities in the labour market and education. The report suggests that,

> Across the professions as a whole, the glass ceiling has been scratched but not broken. The professions still lag way behind the social curve. If anything, the evidence suggests that since 2009, taken as a whole, the professions – despite some pockets of considerable progress – have done too little to catch up. The general picture seems to be of mainly minor changes in the social composition of the professions. At the top especially, the professions remain dominated by a social elite.
> (Milburn, 2012: 3)

The report argues that greater equality needs to be achieved in the labour market.

> The professions have a critical role. They are a key and growing source of employment opportunities. As the society which they serve becomes ever more complex and heterogeneous, the professions themselves will need to keep pace by becoming ever more diverse. In an increasingly competitive global market, they will need to do more to make the most of the widest possible pool of talent.
> (2012: 13)

Research also suggests that inequalities in higher education have a significant impact on social mobility and access to high earning jobs in the labour market (Lindley and Machin, 2013; Sutton Trust, 2013). According to the Sutton Trust,

2 Introduction

> There has also been an increase in the numbers of postgraduates – those staying on in higher education after obtaining their undergraduate degree. 11 per cent of people in work (aged 26–60) in Britain now hold a postgraduate qualification, up from 4 per cent in 1996. In the past, employers used to accept O-levels or A-levels for many jobs. More recently, a Bachelor's degree was expected. Now, graduates seek to distinguish themselves increasingly by acquiring a postgraduate degree. But as the requirements of the labour market have become more demanding, this has exacerbated educational inequalities as workers with postgraduate degrees increasingly come from richer family backgrounds.
>
> (Lindley and Machin, 2013: 5)

The report also suggests that women's increased education has become a key factor in narrowing wage differentials and that,

> These patterns of rising wage differentials for those with the highest levels of education, coupled with rising higher educational inequality by family income, will make it harder to shift the already low levels of social mobility in Britain and America. As educational expectations grow and the economic and social position of workers with no or limited qualifications (especially men) has worsened, the need to improve the education and training of a significant section of the workforce becomes ever more important.
>
> (2013: 5)

The research also suggests that the introduction of tuition fees may impact recruitment patterns in higher education.

> The impact of the new £9000 fee arrangements for undergraduates on the social mix in postgraduate education should be kept under careful review, so that appropriate action can be taken where it can be demonstrated that it is further reducing social mobility. The Office for Fair Access should look at universities' postgraduate recruitment patterns as part of their annual assessment of access agreements, and consider what steps are being taken to ensure a broad social intake. The Higher Education Funding Council for England (HEFCE) should help improve our understanding of postgraduate study and financing by collecting data on fees, costs and the socio-economic background of students.
>
> (2013: 6)

The USA has also seen significant cuts in educational spending with a reduction in teacher pay, a reduction of teaching staff in schools as well as cuts to services for the most disadvantaged members of society (Apple, 2013). Consequently, such a fragile, 'risk' and fractured society leads to greater insecurity and instability in an already threatened world (Beck, 1992). As Apple states in the USA,

> All around us, the effects of such things as unemployment, growing economic inequalities, housing foreclosures, the defunding of programs for the poor, hunger, homelessness, loss of pensions and healthcare, resurgent racism, anti-immigration sentiment and violence and so much more are becoming ever more visible.
>
> (2013: 1)

Apple (2013) suggests that in times of change and insecurity, these disadvantages come to the fore. 'Similar racialising effects are all too visible as well, as choice programs foster a set of strategies in which dominant groups are able to protect their children and themselves from the body and culture of the 'Polluting Other' (Apple, 2013: 7).

Aspects of insecurity are apparent in the creation and existence of an employment culture which has manifested in greater competition for jobs and less collaboration between colleagues and a decrease in collegiality resulting in a 'dog eat dog' mentality (Bhopal and Jackson, 2013). The academy has not escaped this insecurity. Academics all over the world are grappling with significant global changes; full-time permanent contracts are no longer the norm, working conditions have deteriorated, for some, salaries have remained the same and, managerial power and demands for 'accountability' have increased. The introduction of tuition fees in the UK has created a consumerist culture in which universities have to focus on providing students a 'service' that they are paying for. Consequently there is a greater focus on student satisfaction surveys as well as the demands of the Research Excellence Framework (REF)[1] in the UK which positions universities in league tables. Research by Bhopal and Jackson in 2013 which explored the views of thirty-five academics in the UK found that many respondents reported experiencing covert and subtle forms of racism and that the work of White academics was celebrated and profiled compared to that of BME academics. The report also found an underrepresentation of BME staff at the most senior levels and on decision making committees. REF panels were given as an example of this. There were contrasting views on the REF. Some respondents felt that the REF exercise was an objective exercise that 'neutralised ethnicity'. Others suggested that a possible negative effect of the REF was one which emphasised subjectivity in how outputs would be judged and those researching areas such as race, diversity and inclusion may be seen negatively. Other aspects mentioned by respondents in the research were lack of trust in them and a lack of credibility in their work, as well as reporting feeling like 'outsiders' in their own institutions. Some recommendations of the research include: an acknowledgement of discrimination and exclusionary practices that exist for BME academics in higher education, strategies that need to be developed to support the

4 *Introduction*

career promotion and progression of BME staff, and a recognition of the role that BME staff could play in senior management committees and decision making processes. The authors state that there is a greater need for mentoring networks that can provide BME academics the support and advice they need for promotion and career progression. Research also suggests a prevalence of subtle racism in higher education in which BME groups continue to remain excluded and marginalised from senior decision making roles and positions (Bhopal, 2014).

This book explores the experiences of black and minority ethnic groups (BME) in higher education. It examines how their experiences in universities are affected by their identities such as their race, gender and class and how the intersectionality of these identities work to position them as 'outsiders' in the White space of the academy. The book makes a comparison between BME academics in the UK and those in the USA by exploring how their experiences are understood in two different social, economic and political contexts. The empirical data for the book is based on a qualitative study carried out between 2011–2013 in the UK and USA. It is based on thirty-five interviews with respondents who were employed in universities in the UK and thirty who were employed in universities in the USA.

The book aims to:

- Specifically examine areas of discrimination and disadvantage such as race, class and gender in higher education as well as debating the difficulties of such concepts in relation to the experiences of BME academics in higher education.
- Explore how intersectionalities of identity position BME academics in the academy.
- Compare the experiences of academics working in UK and USA universities by analysing contesting discourses of identity in these different social and cultural contexts.

This book provides an original comparative account of racialised and gendered experiences of BME academics in two differing contexts: that of the UK and the USA. It examines the ways in which identities are understood and conceptualised in two different yet similar cultural and political climates. By exploring these identities in the global and local context of higher education, the book bridges a much-needed gap in educational and social scientific research. This book is based on the premise that race is a controversial subject in which difficult and contested discourses are the norm and analyses such discourses through empirical and theoretical debates within educational research to understand issues of race, identity, culture and inclusion.

Chapter 2 *Higher education in the UK and USA* outlines the different higher educational contexts in the UK and USA. It provides contextual detail on how higher education operates in the two different social and political contexts and draws upon previous literature that has explored the experiences of BME academics and provides a critical analysis of the debates and issues as well as an analysis of how these debates are situated within the wider context of the academy.

Chapter 3 *The research and methodology* outlines the research methodology. It explores how respondents participated in in-depth semi-structured interviews which focused on aspects of their experiences of becoming academics and entering the academy; promotion and progression; aspects of career development; the positioning of respondents and how their identities affect their role in the academy; the process of the REF; the impact of financial cuts in higher education institutions and the effect this has on individual career trajectories and the different types of support structures in higher education institutions.

Chapter 4 *Theoretical understandings of identity in the academy* provides a critical understanding of race and identity within the context of higher education. It explores how BME academics are positioned in the academy and how their positioning is affected by aspects of gender, race, class and power. The chapter uses empirical research to examine how identities are translated within the context of higher education and how BME academics understand their own identity within the context of higher education. This chapter focuses on empirical data from respondents who were working in universities in the USA.

Chapter 5 *'Outsiders' in the academy?* explores the position of BME academics in the academy. It specifically examines the 'outsider' status of BME academics in the White space of the academy. The chapter uses empirical findings from the study to explore aspects of power, race, class and gender by comparing the experiences of BME academics in the UK and the USA. It concludes by analysing how a comparative perspective can provide us with an understanding of inclusion for BME academics who are positioned as 'outsiders' in the academy.

Chapter 6 *Climbing the ladder: promotion and progression* concentrates on the career progression of BME academics to provide an understanding of racialised identities in the academy. It explores the discourses by which BME academics negotiate their identities in relation to their career progression and promotion. It does so by examining the different facets and themes of identity within the context of belonging and exclusion within the academy and how these contribute to notions of inclusion and exclusion within the White space of the academy.

Chapter 7 *Inclusion, equality and social justice* explores how BME identities in the academy can be understood in relation to issues of inclusion, equality and social justice. It examines how processes of inclusion and exclusion position BME academics in the academy. The chapter focuses on aspects of inclusive policy making such as the Equality Act 2010 and explores the workings of such policy making in relation to aspects of social justice in the academy; it does so by drawing on theoretical understandings of inclusion and social justice.

Finally, Chapter 8 concludes the book by bringing together previous discussions on the positioning of BME academics in the UK and the USA. It suggests ways in which we can engage in difference in order to move towards greater equity in educational policy making and practice.

Note

1 The Research Excellence Framework is the system of assessing the quality of research in universities in the UK. It is based on a process of expert review in which universities will be assessed on their publications, funding and research impact. The REF is discussed in Chapter 2.

References

Apple, M. (2013) *Can Education Change Society?* London and New York: Routledge.
Beck, U. (1992) *Risk Society: Towards a new modernity*. London: Sage.
Bhopal, K. (2014) *The Experiences of BME Academics in Higher Education: Aspirations in the face of inequality*. London: Leadership Foundation for Higher Education, Stimulus Paper.
Bhopal, K. and Jackson, J. (2013) *The Experiences of Black and Minority Ethnic Academics: Multiple identities and career progression*. Southampton: EPSRC.
Lindley, J. and Machin, S. (2013) *The Postgraduate Premium: Revisiting trends in social mobility and education inequalities in Britain and America*. London: Sutton Trust.
Milburn, A. (2012) *Fair Access to Professional Careers*. London: Crown.

2 Higher education in the UK and USA

This chapter outlines the different higher educational contexts in the UK and USA. It provides details on how higher education operates in these two different social and political contexts. It draws upon previous literature that has explored the experiences of BME academics and provides a critical analysis of the debates and how these are situated within the wider context of the academy.

Inequalities in the labour market

There has been a great deal of research that has explored inequalities in recruitment and selection processes, particularly in relation to candidates' racial and ethnic background (Beattie and Johnson, 2011). Kandola (2009) suggests that individuals are more likely to show bias towards some groups rather than others, particularly in relation to race. Others (Bassanini and Saint-Martin, 2008) suggest that inequalities and bias in the recruitment of those from BME backgrounds demonstrates a continued source of social and economic injustice and Bassanini and Saint-George (2008) argue that those from BME backgrounds continue to face disadvantages in the labour market in terms of access to particular jobs and job security. Similar findings have also been reported in Europe (Lefranc, 2010); New Zealand (Tobias et al., 2008) and North America (Pager et al., 2009). Li and Heath (2009) in their UK research found that BME individuals were more likely to experience higher rates of economic inactivity, earn less per hour and experience lower levels of occupational attainment, and were disadvantaged in all aspects of the labour market, compared to their White colleagues. Research in the USA has also found similar biases, for example those with Anglo-Saxon sounding names were more likely to secure an interview compared to those who had obvious African American names, particularly in cases where the CVs of candidates were identical (Bertrand and Mullainathan, 2004). This was also a finding in research carried out by Dovidio and Gaertner (2000) who found that when Black and White candidates were considered for the same posts, Black candidates were not selected as often as White candidates, even when they had the same qualifications. Rooth states that, 'there are recruiters who implicitly discriminate, but who would not explicitly do so. The results present evidence that recruiting behaviour is being affected by implicit prejudice rather than by explicit discrimination' (2010: 46). Son Hing et al. (2008) suggest that during selection, a process of 'aversive racism' takes place in which interviewers are more likely to remember the negative characteristics of candidates, especially when they are Black, and so are less likely to recommend them for the position. The research suggests that despite the existence of equality policies both in the UK and the USA, those from minority ethnic backgrounds continue to face disadvantages in the labour market.

Diversity in higher education

There is a plethora of research that has explored aspects of institutional racism in higher education (Shiner and Modood, 2002; Law et al., 2004) and much of the research points to the inequalities that students face in higher education institutions. Whilst later research suggests that the numbers of BME students in higher education has increased, there is evidence to suggest that they continue to be disadvantaged. For example, after graduation BME students are more likely to be unemployed and earn less compared to their White counterparts (National Equality Panel, 2010). David Ruebain, head of the Equality Challenge Unit has advised that,

> HEIs [Higher Education Institutions] are increasingly competing in a global market, with a growing diversity of suppliers, including private and other providers. Some would argue that this is not the time to prioritise equality and diversity. *On the contrary, this is the very time to focus on these issues* and not just because the ever-changing national and international context will have consequences for compliance and best practice in the area of equality. Diversity will be important to assist the HE [Higher Education] sector to compete in an increasingly competitive and itself diverse environment.
>
> (Ruebain, 2012: 4, original emphasis)

Ruebain (2012) suggests that as universities continue to compete in the global economic environment, there is pressure on them to cater for a more diverse range of students with a range of differentiated needs and demands. Consequently, the benefits of a diverse workforce will include those who will be in a position to offer a range of skills, experiences and expertise.

> Embedding equality and diversity, particularly within systems, structures, and practices, has the potential to produce huge benefits for society as a whole, contributing new and developing models of economic and social

activity and embedding attitudes that staff and students will carry with them into the wider society.

(Ruebain, 2012: 5)

However, funding changes in education introduced by the Coalition government in England have significantly affected higher education, including cuts to the widening participation agenda (Richardson, 2010). In such a climate of funding cuts, initiatives which tackle inclusion and diversity are the most affected. As Lewis, Hammond and Horvers state,

In these austere times it is easy to see how some Higher Education Institutions especially for those for whom widening participation is no more than a value-added extension of student recruitment activity, may consider widening participation to be one of the first belt loops to be tightened

(2012: 19)

Whilst some universities see the widening participation agenda as a firm commitment to social justice and equality issues, they are at the same time targeting those groups who continue to be disadvantaged in society. Lewis et al. suggest that the danger of such funding cuts may also have severe consequences for other aspects of social justice and inclusion, such as the implementation of the Equality Act 2010.

The Equality Act may encourage or facilitate a complacent approach by managers, administrators and academics to adopt a tick box mentality, leading to an inappropriate preoccupation with figures and audit sheets rather than the broader values, principles and philosophies of widening participation.

(Lewis et al., 2012: 20)

As higher education continues to change and diversify, it will bring with it different challenges, specifically as universities continue to compete for student numbers. The student body will continue to increase in diversity and consequently, higher education institutions have to think about the implementation of different types of inclusive measures to encourage greater attendance from students from non-traditional backgrounds. Research suggests that students from poor and working class backgrounds are less likely to attend research intensive universities (Sutton Trust, 2011). A YouGov poll in 2011 indicated that many individuals feel that those from poorer backgrounds should be given greater support to attend university. Lewis et al. argue that it is the Equality Act that should be used to explore how widening participation can be used to encourage greater inclusion at universities for students from diverse backgrounds. However, senior managers, '... should engage with the philosophy by widening participation through the Equality Act rather than view the Act as merely an additional legislative burden to be overcome' (Lewis et al., 2012: 22).

On the one hand there has been an increase in the numbers of students from a diverse range of ethnic and social backgrounds entering higher education (HESA, 2014) suggesting that widening participation has been addressed, however questions about inclusion, diversity and equality have not been addressed in relation to this (Hey et al., 2011; Bhopal and Jackson, 2013). A failure on the part of organisations to acknowledge and address aspects of inclusion, racism and discrimination continues. Singh states, 'the self-concept that White academics align themselves to – as being "liberal minded rational intellectuals" – coupled with a notion that racism is the product of small minded, morally degenerate individuals is the perfect formula for locating the problem somewhere else' (2009: 6).

Equality in higher education

Equality in higher education has been a concept that has been addressed in different ways. 'We all have an intuitive grasp of the meaning of equality and what it entails. Yet, the more closely we examine it, the more the meaning shifts' (Fredman, 2001: 2). Some research has explored the role of senior managers in setting the agenda for equality in higher education institutions (Crofts and Pilkington, 2012), other research has explored whether equality polices are effective and whether they work in practice for the benefit for those who remain marginalised (Green et al., 2000; Pilkington, 2013). Deem et al. state, 'the extent and importance of managers in higher education has increased considerably in recent years as UK higher education has expanded . . . and the commitment of senior managers to equality of opportunity is clearly of considerable significance' (2005: 82).

Although there has been an increase in the numbers of BME students attending universities, evidence suggests that inequalities in achievement continue to exist (Bhopal and Jackson, 2013). There is also evidence to suggest that those from BME backgrounds are less likely than their White counterparts to attend the most prestigious, research intensive universities (Singh, 2009).

Research (Bhopal and Jackson, 2013) suggests vast inequalities in the experiences of BME academics working in higher education institutions in the UK. Bhopal and Jackson (2013) found that BME academics are more likely to experience covert rather than overt forms of racial discrimination. Bhopal and Jackson (2013) also found in their study that the value of having BME staff in higher education institutions is often unrecognised by senior managers and heads of departments; the work of White (male) academics is profiled and celebrated in institutions rather than that of BME staff; BME staff remain underrepresented at the most senior and decision making levels in higher education institutions and respondents reported that having a more diverse senior management group would have a positive impact on the decision making processes (including those regarding promotion and progression). Findings also suggest that BME academics felt a lack of trust in their abilities and over-scrutinisation of their roles compared to their White colleagues. Respondents also reported contrasting views on the REF and how it worked to assess academic outputs. The Research Excellence Framework (REF) is the system for assessing the quality of research in UK higher education institutions. In 2014, higher education institutions were assessed on the 'excellence' of their research based on a process of expert review. The REF process usually takes place every four years in the UK, although the previous exercise had been in 2008. The assessment of outputs also includes impact case studies and an assessment on the research environment of a university. Universities are graded on the basis of this assessment which determines the amount of funding they receive from HEFCE (Higher Education Funding Council for England). Some BME academics welcomed the REF and saw it as a process of 'neutralising ethnicity', as it was based on objective and clear criteria (the ability to publish and deliver three- and four-star articles assessed by an external body). A possible negative element to the REF was also identified by some respondents which included the fact that articles in some parts of the world such as Africa or the Indian sub-continent were not being recognised or not scoring highly compared to those from the UK and USA.

Respondents in the study also reported experiencing negative views from their students, particularly in relation to their credibility being questioned and judged negatively compared to their White colleagues, as well as having to reach higher thresholds compared to their White colleagues, particularly in terms of promotion and progression. Respondents reported feelings of isolation, marginalisation and exclusion and being an 'outsider' in their institutions. However, some respondents spoke favourably about the existence of mentoring systems which they used as a form of support for their career progression. The report also makes several recommendations for inclusive policy making in higher education, such as an acknowledgement from senior managers that discrimination and exclusionary practices continue to exist in higher education and can have negative impacts on the careers of BME academics; the existence and recognition of unconscious bias towards BME academics, particularly at key career points such as promotion and progression; inclusive strategies to include BME academics staff in higher education institutions to ensure visibility on decision making committees and REF panels. Policy recommendations also include a need to develop formal and informal support networks for BME staff, particularly those who have recently entered higher education. This important piece of research outlines clear issues that BME academics face in higher education and key aspects that need to be addressed if the experiences of BME academics are to be fully included in higher education (Bhopal and Jackson, 2013). Futhermore, Bhopal (2014) argues that higher education institutions state a commitment to diversity through the implementation of a commitment to equality policies, yet there is little evidence to suggest whether the impact of these policies is effective in relation to the inclusion and progression of BME groups in higher education. There is a need for greater comprehensive programmes of targeted action which directly address how the inclusion of BME groups can take place at all levels in higher education institutions. For example it is important that the progression of BME academics is monitored at all academic grades in order that equal access can be achieved to support the career promotion and progression of BME academics. Bhopal and Jackson (2013) suggest that inequalities continue to exist in higher education institutions in the UK and a greater commitment on the part of senior managers and universities is needed to ensure the full inclusion of BME academics. A greater representation of BME academics is needed at senior levels without such appointments being seen as 'token gestures'. The following section will outline equality polices in the UK and how these have worked in higher education institutions.

Universities in the UK

Universities in the UK are regulated by Royal Charter under the Education Reform Act of 1988. There are various different types of universities that exist in the UK. These include ancient universities (founded before 1800); red brick universities (chartered at the beginning of the twentieth century; plate glass universities (chartered after 1966) and 'new' universities (post-1992), those which were former polytechnics or colleges of higher education). These were given university status under the Conservative government led by John Major in 1992, under the Further and Higher Education Act 1992. 'New' universities are teaching rather than research led and focus on vocational education and teaching. Red brick universities also include the Russell Group of universities which are research rather than teaching led. They are a group of 24 universities which in 2012/13 received the highest amount of grant funding from Research Councils in the United Kingdom (RCUK) (House of Commons Business, Innovation and Skills Committee, 2013). Many universities attract overseas students to study at British universities. Universities such as Oxford, Cambridge, Manchester and the London School of Economics rank highly in national and international league tables and are members of the Russell Group. Research suggests that a degree from a Russell Group university is worth considerably more than a degree from another university and those who obtain a degree from a Russell Group university are less likely to be unemployed than those who obtain degrees from other universities (percentage of graduates working in non-graduate jobs, Office for National Statistics, 2013).

The majority of universities are funded by the government. After the Second World War, tuition fees were paid by local education authorities which included fees and maintenance grants. In 1997, with the publication of the Dearing Report, the main recommendation was to end the payment of tuition fees for students and means testing of the maintenance grant. Consequently, a new loans scheme was introduced in 1998. Tuition fees were abolished in England in 1999. In the academic year 2006/7 a new system of tuition fees was introduced in England with variable tuition fees of up to £3000 per year (with the availability of student loans). Tuition fees rose considerably in the academic year 2012/13 with the majority of universities charging £9000 per year.

Staff in higher education

HESA data from 2014 reports that on 1 December 2012 there were 382,515 staff employed in the HE sector (excluding atypical staff), showing an increase of 1.1% from 378,250 staff employed on 1 December 2011. 254,490 staff were employed on full-time contracts (248,125 in 2011) and 128,025 on part-time contracts (130,125 in 2011). A total of 47.1% of full-time staff and 67.3% of part-time staff were female in 2012 showing slight increases in the proportions of female staff from 2011 (46.9% and 67.0% respectively).

On 1 December a total of 48,155 (40.2%) of academic staff were female compared to 80,775 (44.5%) in 2011. 94,600 (51.0%) academic staff were employed on contracts described as having a teaching and research function; 46,795 (25.2%) had an academic employment function described as teaching only. A total of 17,880 academic staff were employed on a contract level described as a professor in 2012; 3870 of these staff were female, representing 21.7%.[1]

BME staff in higher education

The numbers of minority ethnic staff working in higher education institutions in 2012/13 shows that the majority 23.4% were from a Chinese background, 19.2% from an Asian/Asian British Indian background, with a minority from Black/Black British Caribbean (3.4%), Black/Black British African (7.9%) and Asian/Asian British Pakistani (4.8%) and Asian/Asian British Bangladeshi (1.9%) backgrounds.

Table 2.1 Academic staff by academic employment function 2012/13

Activity	Full-time	Part-time	Total
Teaching only	10730	36065	46795
Teaching and research	75710	18890	94600
Research only	34810	7540	42350
Neither teaching or research	1250	590	1840
Total	122500	63085	185585

Source: Higher Education Statistics Agency 2014

Table 2.2 All staff by full-time academic employment, occupational classification and sex 2012/13

Academic contract	Female	% Female	Male	% Male	Total
Managers, directors and senior officials	160	0.1%	270	0.2%	430
Professional occupations	47635	39.7%	73444	54.6%	121085
Associate professional and technical occupations	355	0.3%	625	0.5%	980
Total academic staff	**48155**	**40.2%**	**74345**	**55.2%**	**122500**
Non-academic contract					
Managers, directors and senior officials	4815	4.0%	4935	3.7%	9750
Professional occupations	14025	11.7%	13670	10.2%	27695
Associate professional and technical occupations	15145	12.6%	18220	13.5%	33365
Administrative and secretarial occupations	32240	26.9%	8640	6.4%	40880
Skilled trades occupations	705	0.6%	4705	3.5%	5410
Caring, leisure and other service occupations	1725	1.4%	2090	1.6%	3810
Sales and customer service occupations	690	0.6%	340	0.3%	1035
Process, plant and machine operatives	225	0.2%	1230	0.9%	1455
Total non-academic staff	**71760**	**59.8%**	**60235**	**44.8%**	**131990**
Total staff	**119915**	**100.0%**	**134575**	**100.0%**	**254490**

In this table, 0, 1, and 2 are rounded to 0. All other numbers are rounded up or down to the nearest multiple of 5. Percentages are not subject to rounding.

Source: Higher Education Statistics Agency, 2014.

The numbers of staff from minority ethnic backgrounds in senior management or heads of school functions were low compared to those from White backgrounds. Only 30 were from Black backgrounds, 170 Asian and 85 'other' (HESA, 2014).

The numbers of professors was also low compared to those from White backgrounds, with only 85 who were Black, 950 Asian and 365 'other' (HESA, 2014).

In terms of gender, men were more likely to be in professorial posts compared to women (HESA, 2014).

There are greater numbers of women in higher education and there have been significant advances in the inclusion of women at senior levels in leadership roles (Lumby, 2012). However, the numbers of women who are professors and their representation at the most senior levels (such as for example as Pro-Vice Chancellors and Chancellors) remains low (Breakwell

Table 2.3 Academic staff by ethnic minority group 2012/13, all staff (excluding atypical)

Academic staff	Number	Percentage
Black or Black British-Caribbean	750	3.4%
Black or Black British-African	1730	7.9%
Other Black background	260	1.2%
Asian or Asian British – Indian	4215	19.2%
Asian or Asian British – Pakistani	1045	4.8%
Asian or Asian British – Bangladeshi	410	1.9%
Chinese	5150	23.4%
Other Asian background	3050	13.9%
Other (including mixed)	5375	24.4%
Total	21985	100.0%

In this table, 0, 1, 2 are rounded to 0. All other numbers are rounded up or down to the nearest multiple of 5. Percentages are not subject to rounding.

Source: Higher Education Statistics Agency 2014.

Table 2.4 Academic staff at senior management or heads of schools/functions by ethnicity 2012/13

Ethnicity	Senior Management	Heads of Schools/Functions	Total
White	1355	3780	**5135**
Black	5	25	**30**
Asian	40	130	**170**
Other (including mixed)	20	65	**85**
Unknown	55	185	**240**
Total	**1470**	**4185**	**5655**

Source: Higher Education Statistics Agency 2014

Table 2.5 Academic professors by ethnicity 2012/13

Ethnicity	Total
White	15200
Black	85
Asian	950
Other (including mixed)	365
Unknown	1280
Total	**17880**

Source: Higher Education Statistics Agency 2014

Table 2.6 Academic professors by gender 2012/13

Gender	Professor	Other academic	Total academic
Female	3870	78795	82670
% female	21.7%	47.0%	44.5%
Male	14010	88905	102915
% male	78.3%	53.0%	55.5%
Total	17880	167700	185585

Source: Higher Education Statistics Agency 2014

and Tytherleigh, 2008; HESA, 2014). Furthermore, those from BME backgrounds as less likely to be in decision making roles; their representation at senior levels (such as professors and senior managers) is almost non-existent at Pro-Vice Chancellor and Chancellor levels compared to their White counterparts (ECU, 2011; HESA, 2014).

Research carried out by the University and College Union (UCU, 2012) suggests that even when BME applicants apply for professorial grades; they are less likely to be successful compared to their White counterparts. For example, White applicants were three times more likely to be successful in securing and gaining a professorial position compared to their BME colleagues. Indeed, the UCU suggests that the collection of data on equality and diversity should be used to analyse the disadvantages experienced by those from BME backgrounds. 'Collating and retaining equality data in relation to recruitment and promotion exercises is essential and can help an institution to see whether problems are being caused by lack of applications or lack of success in recruitment or promotion exercises' (UCU, 2012: 19).

Research has also found that there is a considerable pay gap in the payment of male and female professors (Times Higher Education, 2012), and research by the UCU also suggests that this may also be the case in relation to race and ethnicity. According to the UCU,

> For the UK as a whole, Black professors earned 9.4% less than their White colleagues, Chinese professors earned 6.7% less, and other ethnicities including mixed race earned 3.5% less; Asian professorial staff earned 4.0% more than their White counterparts.
> (UCU, 2012: 22)

This finding by the UCU is important because it points to the personal, ad hoc arrangements some institutions are able to offer professors, particularly in the light of 'poaching' exercises for the forthcoming REF (Bhopal, 2013; Times Higher Education, 2013).

UCU believes that the systems for remuneration for professorial (and other senior) staff in many HEIs also contribute to the pay gaps among the professoriate. Ad hoc, opaque and personally negotiated pay arrangements for professorial staff are in direct opposition to transparent and fair professorial grading structures that will deliver on an institution's equal pay obligations. We [UCU] believe that all pay systems should be transparent and equality-proofed and are therefore calling on the sector to negotiate with the recognised trade unions on the introduction of transparent and fair pay structures for professorial staff.

(2012: 23)

Vast inequalities in pay structures continue to exist in higher education institutions and must be addressed for equality of opportunity to be achieved.

Students in higher education

The total number of students who were enrolled in higher education institutions in 2012/13 was 2,340,275, a decrease of 6.3% from 2011/12. This reflects a general decline across the sector in all modes and levels of study which coincides with changes in tuition fees. Postgraduate enrolments decreased by 5.6% and undergraduate enrolments decreased by 6.4% between 2011/12 and 2012/13. Full-time enrolments decreased by 2.3% while part-time enrolments showed a sharper decline of 15.1% over the same period (HESA, 2014).

A total of 2.38 million students were studying for a qualification at 161 higher education institutions in 2012/13. Of these institutions, 160 were publicly funded and one, the University of Buckingham, was privately funded.[2] In 2012/13 a total of 787,900 qualifications were awarded at higher education level to students in publicly funded higher education institutions (together with the University of Buckingham). Of these, 33.3% were at postgraduate level, 51.2% were undergraduate first degree qualifications and 15.5% were other undergraduate qualifications. 25,240 foundation degrees were awarded, which was 3.2% of the total (HESA, 2014).

Minority ethnic students

HESA data suggests that participation in higher education for minority ethnic students continues to increase overall. The following table shows the percentages of first year UK minority ethnic students by mode and level of study.

In the last twenty years there have been significant changes in higher education, particularly in relation to the inclusion of BME groups. Educational attainment has shown an increase amongst ethnic groups, particularly due to an improvement in access to education and an increasing number of BME individuals who are educated in the UK (Simpson et al., 2006). This is also related to positive employment and income outcomes for BME groups

Table 2.7 Percentage of first year UK ethnic minority students in higher education by level and mode of study 2012/13

Type of degree	Ethnic minority
Higher degree (research)	
Full-time	16.5%
Part-time	17.2%
Total higher degree (research)	**16.7%**
Higher degree (taught)	
Full-time	26.7%
Part-time	18.1%
Total higher degree (taught)	**22.4%**
Other postgraduate	
Full-time	15.3%
Part-time	17.6%
Total other postgraduate	**16.7%**
First degree	
Full-time	23.6%
Part-time	13.5%
Total first degree	**22.2%**
Other undergraduate	
Full-time	21.6%
Part-time	13.8%
Total other undergraduate	**15.2%**
All levels	
Full-time	23.0%
Part-time	15.1%
Total all levels	**20.1%**

Percentages are not subject to rounding.

Source: Higher Education Statistics Agency 2014.

(Clark and Drinkwater, 2007). Data produced from an analysis of the 2011 census suggests that those from BME backgrounds were more likely than their White counterparts to have a degree level qualification or equivalent (Lymperopoulou and Parameshwaran, 2014). In 2011, those from White Gypsy or Irish Traveller, Pakistani, Bangladeshi and White and Black Caribbean groups were less likely to have degree level qualifications (or the equivalent) compared to those from Chinese (43%), Indian (42%) and Black African (40%) backgrounds (Lymperopoulou and Parameshwaran, 2014). The most disadvantaged group in terms of obtaining degree level qualifications (or their equivalent) were the White Gypsy or Irish Traveller groups (60%), followed by White Irish (29%), Bangladeshi (29%), Pakistani (28%) and White British (24%) groups. The authors suggest,

> This partly reflects the different age composition of these groups and the lower rates of participation in education among some ethnic minority

women. For example the White Irish group have an older age structure than other groups, while Pakistani and Bangladeshi women are less likely to have qualifications than women belonging to other ethnic groups due to earlier marriage, family formation and cultural practices.
(Lymperopoulou and Parameshwaran, 2014: 2)

The research suggests that '... across all age groups members of ethnic minority groups were more likely to have degree level qualifications than people in the White British group' (Lymperopoulou and Parameshwaran, 2014: 3). This research confirms that there are vast differences in the educational achievement of different BME groups in higher education institutions in the UK.

Research also suggests differences between minority ethnic groups in the types of higher education institutions they attend. The Elevation Networks Trust (2012) suggests that there are more Black students studying for various subjects and degrees at the University of East London (UK) than in the top twenty UK higher education institutions combined. The competition for graduates to enter the labour market has increased, resulting in greater competition for jobs, with the majority of employers expecting applicants to have obtained an upper second class degree (Snowden, 2012). Inequalities in access to different types of universities continue:

children with professional parents in the UK, Australia and the US are approximately three times more likely to enter a high-status university (rather than one with lower status) than those with working-class parents. While attainment in secondary education accounts for most of the gap in participation at the top universities, more than a quarter of the difference remains unexplained. This suggests that there are significant numbers of working class children who, even though they have the academic ability to attend, choose to enter a non-selective institution instead.
(Jerrim in O'Leary, 2013: 3)

Equality policies in the UK

The Macpherson report which was published in 1999 was the result of the inquiry into the racist murder of the teenager Stephen Lawrence in 1993. The report findings suggested that the police were 'institutionally racist' and these findings had a significant impact on how race relations were subsequently understood in England. The inquiry led to changes in the Race Relations (Amendment) Act 2000 which gave public bodies such as schools a legal duty to report and record all racist incidents in order that such data could be collected and monitored. The Act also included a public duty for all institutions to promote race equality in which organisations had to address discrimination as well as introduce diversity and race awareness training for their workforce.

However, the Coalition government which came into power in England in May 2010 introduced changes in legislation that meant that organisations were no longer required to record or monitor racist incidents. New powers for schools and education were introduced under the Equality Act and OFSTED[3] guidelines. A new public sector equality duty was introduced in April 2011 as part of the general equality duty (section 149 of the Equality Act 2010). In line with the general equality duty, public sector organisations have due regard for the need to:

- Eliminate unlawful discrimination, harassment and victimisation and other conduct prohibited by the Act.
- Advance equality of opportunity between people who share a protected characteristic and those who do not.
- Foster good relations between people who share a protected characteristic and those who do not.

The Equality Act considers aspects of advancing equality through:

- Removing or minimising disadvantages suffered by people due to their protected characteristics.
- Taking steps to meet the needs of people from protected groups where these are different from the needs of other people.
- Encouraging people from protected groups to participate in public life or in other activities where their participation is disproportionately low.[4]

The Equality Act encourages positive relations by tackling prejudice and promoting greater understanding between individuals from different groups. The new duty covers protected characteristics such as age, disability, gender reassignment, pregnancy and maternity, race, religion or belief, sex and sexual orientation. According to the Equality and Human Rights Commission,

> The general equality duty therefore requires organisations to consider how they could positively contribute to the advancement of equality and good relations. It requires equality considerations to be reflected into the design of policies and the delivery of services, including internal policies, and for these issues to be kept under review. Compliance with the general equality duty is a legal obligation.[5]

The Equality Act 2010 also refers to victimisation and harassment and

> the duties provide a framework to help institutions tackle persistent and long-standing issues of disadvantage, such as gender stereotyping in subject choice, attainment gaps between White and Black and minority ethnic students and low participation rates of disabled people. They also provide a strategic and systematic means of tackling major entrenched disadvantage across the sector.[6]

Whilst the Equality Act is a positive step forward in addressing inequalities in the workplace, questions remain on how it works in practice and the impact it has on tackling cultural change in organisations such as fostering greater inclusion and diversity of BME and minority groups at senior management levels. Crofts and Pilkington state that, ' . . . the equality duties and the requirement to conduct equality analyses (formerly Equality Impact Assessments) require a consideration and demonstration of equality outcomes, and a more detailed understanding of notions relating to substantive equality (such as disproportionate adverse impact)' (2012: 12). There is also research to suggest that senior managers do not understand how diversity works in practice and how their organisations should in fact deal with it (Deem et al., 2005; Crofts and Pilkington, 2012). If this is indeed the case, whether the aims of the Equality Act will be achieved is highly questionable. Research has also suggested that there are great discrepancies between the views of individual staff and senior managers when addressing aspects of inequality,

> where equality issues are more visible and where for example, you have a high number of BME students, equality issues are more pronounced. However, this perception does not sit comfortably with the perception of some staff and students within the institution, who have pointed to a number of areas which they feel demonstrate either instances of discrimination, or at the very least, a failure by the institution to take equality issues seriously, even when the data suggests there may be a problem.
> (Crofts and Pilkington, 2012: 26–27)

Research conducted in 2012 by the University and College Union (UCU) suggests that 'Forty-two years on from the first legislation on equal pay, and some ten years since the first positive equality requirements for public bodies, it is clear we still have a long way to go' (UCU, 2012: 1).

Other researchers have questioned the value of diversity and policy documents and explored whether policy such as that enshrined in the Equality Act is of value when addressing aspects of inequality and marginalisation for minority groups. Ahmed for example suggests that, ' . . . rather than assuming that such documents do what they say . . . we need to follow such documents around, examine how they get taken up' (Ahmed, 2007: 590). Ahmed is critical of the value of such documents and suggests that their use may conceal the racism that takes place in some organisations and that the use of documents is not necessarily a sign that aspects of racism have been dealt with. ' . . . how documents are taken up as signs of good performance, as expressions of commitment and as descriptors of organisations as "being" diverse . . . such documents work to conceal forms of racism when they get taken up this way' (2007: 590). Ahmed also questions who controls the writing of such equality documents and the effect this has on how they are translated and used in practice. Equality documents may be used to demonstrate that organisations are dealing with aspects of inequality, racism and diversity when in fact a *commitment* to anti-racism does not necessarily indicate that racism and exclusion is being dealt with. 'The politics of diversity has become what we call "image management"; diversity work is about generating the "right image" and correcting the wrong one' (Ahmed, 2007: 605). Ahmed also examines how the identity of Whiteness contributes to the process by which diversity is understood in organisations. 'Diversity work becomes *about changing perceptions of whiteness rather than changing the whiteness of organisations*. Doing well, or a good performance, would then be about being perceived as a diverse organisation' (Ahmed, 2007: 605 original emphasis).

Athena SWAN

Athena SWAN is a charter mark that was introduced by the Equality Challenge Unit (ECU) in June 2005 as a UK wide initiative. It is a charter that recognises the good practice that some institutions have introduced regarding the inclusion of women in Science, Technology, Engineering, Medicine and Mathematics (STEMM) subjects. For universities to receive gold, silver or bronze awards they must be able to demonstrate how their institutions are providing support for the inclusion and progression of women in these subjects. They must also demonstrate how their organisations are contributing to change to include a gender balance in decision making processes. David Ruebain head of the ECU states, 'Through this process, Athena SWAN has been transformative in addressing the underrepresentation of women in senior academic positions in SET (Science, Engineering and Technology) departments' (Ruebain, 2012: 5). Clearly the Athena SWAN charter has made a significant difference to the inclusion of women in STEMM subjects, particularly as there has been an increase in the numbers of organisation agreeing to participate in the charter. Such participation also demonstrates a clear commitment to gender equity issues and a move towards increasing the representation of women in STEMM subjects at senior levels. Those institutions which hold gold awards must be able to demonstrate a substantial and well-established activity and achievement record in working towards equality in career progression in STEMM subjects; they must also demonstrate a clear initiative to increase the numbers of women who represent these areas and demonstrate beacon activities in gender equality to the wider community.[7] The beliefs underpinning the charter include: the advancement of STEMM internationally; the adequate representation of women in these traditionally male dominated areas, and an equal benefit for men and women to participate in these subjects. Morley states, 'Universities need to be held to account for their low numbers of senior women' and also that universities should be barred from research funding unless they can prove they are supporting female academics' careers.[8] She has also suggested that higher education institutions should be compelled to sign up to the Athena SWAN project so that 'gender [is] factored into all strategic planning and processes'.[9]

Gender equality charter mark

The gender equality charter mark was introduced in 2014 by the Equality Challenge Unit. Its aim is to address gender inequalities in the workplace, particularly higher education institutions, and to explore imbalances in the arts, humanities and social sciences. It also aims to challenge the underrepresentation of women in senior roles in these subject areas. The gender equality charter mark is not just confined to addressing inequalities for academic staff but also extends to professional and support staff and includes both men and women, and those who define themselves as transgender. It is an extension of the Athena SWAN charter. The Equality Challenge Unit will aim to ultimately bring together both the Athena SWAN charter and the gender equality charter mark. The Equality Challenge Unit has been involved in a consultation exercise (May 2014) to enhance and develop the gender equality charter mark. 'The model encourages change at department, school and institutional levels. It is concerned with long-term culture change which will benefit all staff and students. The framework will be developed to take into account the context of non-STEMM disciplines' (ECU consultation document 2013: 2).

The Equality Challenge Unit considered whether an overarching scheme on addressing inequalities which covered all protected characteristics in the workplace would be just as effective but they found that (ECU Gender Equality Charter Mark Framework 2014: 2):

1 An overall scheme could lose the characteristic-specific focus needed to make real and lasting change.
2 It could potentially prevent institutions from targeting individual priority areas based on their local context.
3 Schemes already exist covering some protected characteristics, so an overall scheme would duplicate existing activity undertaken by some institutions.
4 A large scheme would increase the demands on equality and diversity staff, with higher time and resource implications than smaller, more focused schemes, and
5 There would also be high resource implications for ECU in developing and administering an overall scheme.

In June 2013, the Equality Challenge Unit consulted the higher education sector on the development of the gender equality charter mark. They received 120 responses to their survey of which 71% of respondents were likely or very likely to apply as a member of the charter and 5% of respondents were unlikely or very unlikely to apply.[10] The Equality Challenge Unit stresses that such exercises are not simply tick box exercises and that it is important for institutions to ensure that they invest time in advancing equality and taking actions to improve inequalities in their organisations, rather than merely reporting on it. At the same time, such schemes have to be flexible and not place burdens on organisations. However, those who have already participated in Athena SWAN can build on the mechanisms and processes which should already be in place for some organisations. However, all institutions are required to collect and analyse staff data on gender and ethnicity in order to comply with the Equality Act and they are also required to submit data on staff to HESA on an annual basis. Consequently, institutions can use the charter mark to meet their main objectives for achieving gender equality.

Race equality charter mark

As a result of the success of the Athena SWAN charter, the Equality Challenge Unit is developing a race equality charter which will lead to systemic change to progress race equality in organisations and which will help institutions to advance race equality in their institutions. The race equality charter will include a framework which will address race equality in the workplace and explore how institutions are addressing race equality. This mechanism will force institutions to outline how they will specifically address aspects of race equality in the same ways in which gender inequalities have been challenged through the Athena SWAN charter. Whilst such a charter mark is to be welcomed, the Equality Challenge Unit argues, as it does for the gender equality charter mark, that it is important that it is not a tick box exercise. One of the positive aspects includes forcing institutions to think about race equality issues in ways similar to those in which gender has been recognised as a possible means of discrimination against women. It will also need to contribute to organisational and institutional change in which practical measures can be advanced such as the inclusion of BME groups at senior professorial levels and representations in decision making forums. It must lead to instigating some change in organisations as well as a recognition that race remains a key factor of disadvantage, particularly at key career trajectories such as promotion and progression (Bhopal, 2014). The Equality Challenge Unit states,

> There are positives and negatives to any charter mark. ECU does not want to develop a box-ticking exercise or anything which is overly prescriptive. At the same time, any charter mark needs to be robust and only institutions which are actively addressing racial inequalities should achieve a standard.[11]

The race equality charter mark will be introduced in 2015. The Equality Challenge Unit states,

> Race equality has specific challenges and issues within higher education and society more generally, which have implications for the approach a charter mark needs to take. People are still much less comfortable talking about race equality than they are gender equality. In addition, race involves minority groups, whereas improving gender equality involves a group which represents at least half of the population (although women are still a minority in the political sense).
>
> (Equality Charter Marks, 2013: 6)

The Equality Challenge Unit points out the need for a specific charter mark which addresses race because:

1 Race is an incredibly complicated area and one where for too long we have been referring to black and minority ethnic (BME) people as a homogenous group. We know that the higher education landscape is very different for different minority ethnic groups and the different issues and barriers which exist for those groups need to be considered.
2 Geographical and local contexts are important considerations. Some regions and areas have much higher BME populations than others, which will have an impact on the diversity of staff recruited from the local area. The Equality Challenge Unit argues that there are different ways in which data on race is presented in organisations and some are not appropriate to address race equality.

(Equality Charter Marks, 2013: 6)

The race equality charter mark will be based on specific targets for organisations which will explore the progress they have made in relation to addressing race inequalities in their organisations and are particularly focused around a long term culture change in organisations which will address race inequalities. Similarly to the gender equality charter mark, the race equality charter mark will apply to academics and those working in professional and support roles and will also address race inequality for students. 'A significant part of the charter mark will involve addressing 'pipeline issues', things which might prevent BME students from progressing into postgraduate study and employment within academia' (Equality Charter Marks, 2013: 7).

International experiences of higher education

South Africa

Research in South Africa has explored the experiences of BME academics in international contexts, particularly in relation to how they manage their identities and aspects of their career progression, as well as how BME academics position themselves in the academy compared to their White colleagues. Jawitz (2012) argues that in the South African context there has been a masking of issues to do with race and exclusion in the South African political and social climate. Jawitz's research (2012) suggests a silencing of issues to do with race and consequently it is difficult to understand how discourses of race and exclusion are understood within the South African higher education context. Jawitz suggests that the study of race is not considered to be worthy of attention in higher education and consequently it is ignored and there is a need for institutions to maintain a notion of 'cultural safety' with issues concerning race (Tolich, 2002). Consequently, the challenge for understanding race in higher education in South Africa is that it 'continues to be a highly radicalised space' (Jawitz, 2012: 547).

Dixson and Rousseau (2005), however, suggest that race has to be addressed in the South African context, otherwise a 'colour blind' perspective will continue to emphasise Whiteness as the norm in the White space of the academy in which the study of race will remain insignificant. Critical Race Theory has been used to explain how Whiteness as a dominant ideology continues in the White space of the academy. The use of narratives in the approach taken by critical race theorists emphasises how the lives of non-White individuals should be central in exploring the discourses of marginalisation, racism and exclusion – particularly in relation to their experiences in higher education (Yosso, 2005).

Schulze's research (2005) suggests that Black academics in the South African context report a heavy teaching load compared to their colleagues and the need for a supportive work environment in which mentoring systems would be beneficial for their progression to senior positions. Research also suggests that female academics in South Africa report challenges to their position in relation to promotion and progression to senior academic roles (Singh et al., 1995) and that men are more satisfied with their pay levels than women (Tang and Talpade, 1999). However, women are more likely to rely on external support (such as friends and family) compared to their male colleagues (Olsen et al., 1995). Acker and Feuerverger (1996) suggest that female academics feel they have to provide a greater nurturing role to students and other female colleagues compared to their male colleagues. Others have stressed that Black academics feel they are viewed by their colleagues in stereotypical ways and that this works to disadvantage them in the academy, particularly in relation to performance and career progression (Niemann and Dovidio (1998). Furthermore, there is evidence to suggest that those working in traditionally Black universities report high levels of job satisfaction and greater collaboration with their colleagues (Okolo and Eddy, 1994). Indeed, institutional racism has been a key factor that has been identified in South African universities in relation to equity, pay and inclusion (Gwele, 2002).

Canada

Research in Canada which has explored the experiences of Black female academics suggests that women use different types of support mechanisms to ensure their success: this is often related to their own self-reliance and how they cope with stereotypical images of themselves as 'Black women' (Wane, 2009). However, Black women emphasise how their work in the academy has significant benefits for their communities beyond the working environment. 'Most women emphasised education as one of the transformative tools within their communities and many felt it was one of the vehicles through which they could dismantle and transform the social and political barriers for Black people' (Wane, 2009: 65). However, Tierney (1993) suggests that Black women in the Canadian context continue to be positioned as outsiders in the academy and struggle with their credibility in which they constantly have to justify their position in the academy to their White colleagues (Wane, 2009). Adeleye-Fayemi (2004) suggests however, that Black women can also examine how they can reclaim the White space of the academy in order that they can be empowered. Patricia Hill Collins (1990) has suggested that Black women's scholarship can contribute to their empowerment in the academy which they can use to resist oppression. Collins (1990) recognises that Black women are positioned as 'outsiders-within' in the academy. 'It is through this power of self-definition that Black women intellectuals have explored this private, hidden space of their consciousness that allows them to cope with, and in many cases, transcend the confines of gender, class and race oppression' (Collins, 1990: 92–93).

Henry et al. (2013) suggest that Black and minority groups remain marginalised in higher education in Canada as they are positioned as inferior by dominant powerful groups:

> Dominant groups construct/represent/undervalue racialised bodies with the result that they are hired in disproportionately lower numbers, thereby diminishing the value and important dimensions of the teaching and learning process that can be achieved by having faculty with wide ranging diverse backgrounds.
>
> (2013: 6)

Indeed, Black academics are also more likely to experience racism and discrimination from staff and students in the Canadian context.

Caribbean

Research exploring the experiences of Black women academics in the Caribbean suggests that women make greater sacrifices for their families and their children compared to men (Senior, 1990). Gregory (2006) suggests that race, class and gender have significant impacts on the positioning of Black Caribbean women in universities. Gregory (2006) reports that Black women academics are more likely to have heavier teaching loads and serve on more committees compared to Black men. Many of the women reported the lack of opportunity to apply for promotion and progression to senior management roles and tenure compared to their male colleagues.

Equality in the USA

The USA has had different experiences of equality compared to the UK, particularly in terms of employment law regarding the inclusion of Black African Americans[12] and other minority ethnic groups. There have been legal regulations that have been introduced in line with *Brown v. Brown Board of Education*, 1954 and Title VII of the Civil Rights Act of 1964. Such changes in legislation indicated that inequalities in education (and elsewhere) based on racial differences needed to be addressed. Title VII of the Civil Rights Act of 1964 indicates that in employment law individuals cannot be discriminated against due to their race or colour. All employment organisations are expected to comply with this ruling. Kaplin and Lee (1995) suggest that this legal ruling is effective in ensuring that there is no intentional or unintentional discrimination which may take place in the work environment and individuals cannot be excluded from certain types of positions based on their racial or ethnic background. Whilst this ruling has been positive for the inclusion of Black and other minority groups in the workforce, there is evidence to suggest that racial discrimination continues to persist in all sectors of the labour market, particularly education (Jackson, 2008). There is also evidence to suggest an increase in the numbers of complaints of racial discrimination in the labour market (Williams and Williams, 2006).

Universities in the USA

The system of higher education in the USA is very different to that of the UK. The USA is known for having some of the top ranking and most prestigious universities in the world such as Harvard, Yale and Princeton, amongst others. The system of higher education in the USA consists of public, private, liberal arts colleges and community colleges. Public universities are those which are funded through government means. Public universities are state funded and every US state will have at least one public university and some will have significantly more. Some state universities are prestigious, selective and included in the top tier in league tables such as the University of California which includes Berkeley and Los Angeles campuses. Many of the public universities started as teacher training colleges which were then expanded into larger comprehensive state universities which included a range of different subjects offered to students. Generally, those students who reside in the state in which they want to attend university are charged lower fees for public universities compared to those who live out of state. The US government recognises that individuals who already reside in the state in which they want to attend university have contributed through the payment of their taxes to the university compared to those who do not live in the state.

Public universities rely on financial subsidies from state government as well as external support from sponsors. Private universities in the USA are not funded by state governments. Many however, receive tax and other breaks from state governments including student loans and grants. There are different types of private universities in the USA: those which operate on non-profit means and others which run as businesses. The most prestigious private universities include Harvard, Yale and Princeton. Some private universities may be affiliated to religious organisations, such as Brigham

Young University and Duke University. Private universities can set their own admissions policies and tuition fees tend to be much higher at private universities compared to public universities.

Higher education in the USA

The pattern of higher education in the USA has shown a steady increase in the last ten years. Data from the National Centre for Educational Statistics suggests that from 1999–2000 to 2009–10, the percentage of degrees obtained by women remained between approximately 60 and 62% for associate's degrees and between 57 and 58% for bachelor's degrees. In contrast, the percentages of master's and doctor's degrees obtained by women increased from 1999–2000 to 2009–10 (from 58 to 60% and from 45 to 52%, respectively). Within each racial group, women earned the majority of degrees at all levels in 2009–10. The data shows that amongst US residents, Black women earned 68% of associate's degrees, 66% of bachelor's degrees, 71% of master's degrees, and 65% of all doctorate degrees. Hispanic women obtained 62% of associate's degrees, 61% of bachelor's degrees, 64% of master's degrees, and 55% of doctorates.[13]

From 1999–2000 to 2009–10, the number of degrees obtained amongst all US residents increased for students of all racial/ethnic groups for each level of degree, but at varying rates. For associate's, bachelor's, and master's degrees, the change in percentage distribution of degree recipients was marked by an increase in the numbers of degrees awarded to Black and Hispanic students. For doctorate degrees, the change in the percentage distribution of degree recipients was marked by an increase in the number of degrees awarded to Hispanic and Asian/Pacific Islander students.[14]

Amongst US residents, the number of associate degrees awarded to Hispanic students more than doubled from 1999–2000 to 2009–10 (increasing by 118%), and the number earned by Black students increased by 89%. As a result, Black students were awarded 14% and Hispanic students were awarded 13% of all associate degrees in 2009–10, which showed an increase from 11% and 9%, respectively, in 1999–2000. During the same time period, the number of bachelor's degrees awarded to Black students increased by 53%, and the number awarded to Hispanic students increased by 87%. In 2009–10, Black students earned 10% and Hispanics earned 9% of all bachelor's degrees conferred, compared to the 9 and 6%, respectively, earned in 1999–2000. Similarly, the numbers of master's degrees awarded to Black and Hispanic students more than doubled from 1999–2000 to 2009–10 (increasing by 109% and 125%, respectively). As a result, amongst US residents in 2009–10, Black students earned 12% and Hispanics earned 7% of all master's degrees, up from 9% and 5%, respectively, in 1999–2000. The number of doctorate degrees awarded increased by 60% for Hispanic students and by 47% for Black students (U.S. Department of Education, 2012).

Table 2.8 Number of degrees conferred by race/ethnicity (USA)

Number of degrees conferred to U.S. residents by degree-granting institutions, percentage distribution of degrees conferred, and percentage of degrees conferred to females, by level of degree and race/ethnicity: Academic years 1999–2000 and 2009–10

Level of degree and race/ethnicity	Number		Percentage distribution		Percent conferred to females	
	1999–2000	2009–10	1999–2000	2009–10	1999–2000	2009–10
Associate's	554,845	833,337	100.0	100.0	60.3	62.0
White	408,772	552,863	73.7	66.3	59.8	60.9
Black	60,221	113,905	10.9	13.7	65.2	68.3
Hispanic	51,573	112,211	9.3	13.5	59.4	62.4
Asian/Pacific Islander	27,782	44,021	5.0	5.3	56.8	58.5
American Indian/Alaska Native	6,497	10,337	1.2	1.2	65.8	64.9
Bachelor's	1,198,809	1,602,480	100.0	100.0	57.5	57.4
White	929,106	1,167,499	77.5	72.9	56.6	56.0
Black	108,013	164,844	9.0	10.3	65.7	65.9
Hispanic	75,059	140,316	6.3	8.8	59.6	60.7
Asian/Pacific Islander	77,912	117,422	6.5	7.3	54.0	54.5
American Indian/Alaska Native	8,719	12,399	0.7	0.8	60.3	60.7
Master's	406,761	611,693	100.0	100.0	60.0	62.6
White	324,981	445,038	79.9	72.8	59.6	61.8
Black	36,595	76,458	9.0	12.5	68.2	71.1
Hispanic	19,384	43,535	4.8	7.1	60.1	64.3
Asian/Pacific Islander	23,538	42,072	5.8	7.0	52.0	54.3
American Indian/Alaska Native	2,263	3,960	0.6	0.6	62.7	64.3
Doctor's[1]	106,494	140,505	100.0	100.0	47.0	53.3
White	82,984	104,426	77.9	74.3	45.4	51.4
Black	7,080	10,417	6.6	7.4	61.0	65.2
Hispanic	5,039	8,085	4.7	5.8	48.4	55.0
Asian/Pacific Islander	10,684	16,625	10.0	11.8	48.8	56.5
American Indian/Alaska Native	707	952	0.7	0.7	52.9	54.8

[1] Includes Ph.D., Ed.D., and comparable degrees at the doctoral level. Includes most degrees formerly classified as first-professional, such as M.D., D.D.S., and law degrees.

Source: U.S. Department of Education, National Center for Education Statistics. (2012). *The Condition of Education 2012* (NCES 2012-045), Table A-47-2.

Black staff in USA higher education

In 2011, of those full-time faculty whose race/ethnicity was known, 79% were White (44% were White males and 35% were White females), 6% were Black, 4% were Hispanic, 9% were Asian/Pacific Islander, and less than 1% were American Indian/Alaska Native or two or more races. Amongst full-time professors, 84% were White (60% were White males and 25% were White females), 4% were Black, 3% were Hispanic, 8% were Asian/Pacific Islander, and less than 1% were American Indian/Alaska Native (U.S. Department of Education, 2013).

There is a plethora of research exploring the experiences of academics in universities in the USA. Much of the research points to aspects of racism, exclusion and marginalisation centring on the experiences of Black African American academics. Olsen et al. (1995) suggest that a process of 'symbolic racism' takes place which, ' . . . denounces overt forms of prejudice while denying access to resources, information and sources of support (many of which are informal) essential to success' (1995: 271). Riggins argues that racism takes place indirectly and covertly which is, 'conveyed primarily through subtleties of face to face interaction such as hostile staring, silence, joking and labelling' (Riggins, 2001: 1). Weber and Vandeyar (2008) suggest that when Black African American academics experience racism, they are more likely to leave their institution (a process of flight), particularly if they are positioned as 'outsiders' in the White domain of the academy (Gwele, 2002).

Research has also outlined the prevalence of gender differences in the experiences of Black African American academics in higher education. Black African American women are more likely to be concentrated in lower grades in universities, report lower salary grades, heavy teaching loads and less time to spend on research compared to Black and White men (Allen et al., 2000; Olsen et al., 1995). Many Black African American women continue to report feelings of isolation, exclusion and marginalisation in their experiences of working in universities in the USA, and the need for greater support and mentoring systems to advance their careers (Steward et al., 1995).

Jackson's research (2008) also suggests significant gender differences in the experiences of Black African American academics working in universities in the USA. He argues that whilst there is a great deal of discrimination in the labour market directed towards Black African Americans in general, it is Black African American men who remain disadvantaged compared to Black African American women; they are less likely to be employed in prestigious universities compared to Black African American women and their White counterparts. Jackson suggests that, 'It is quite possible that implicit discriminatory practices in higher education produce race segregation' (2008: 1005) and that there are particular processes involved in gaining employment which are often related to the use and availability of 'academic gatekeeper processes'. These are specific mechanisms which exists

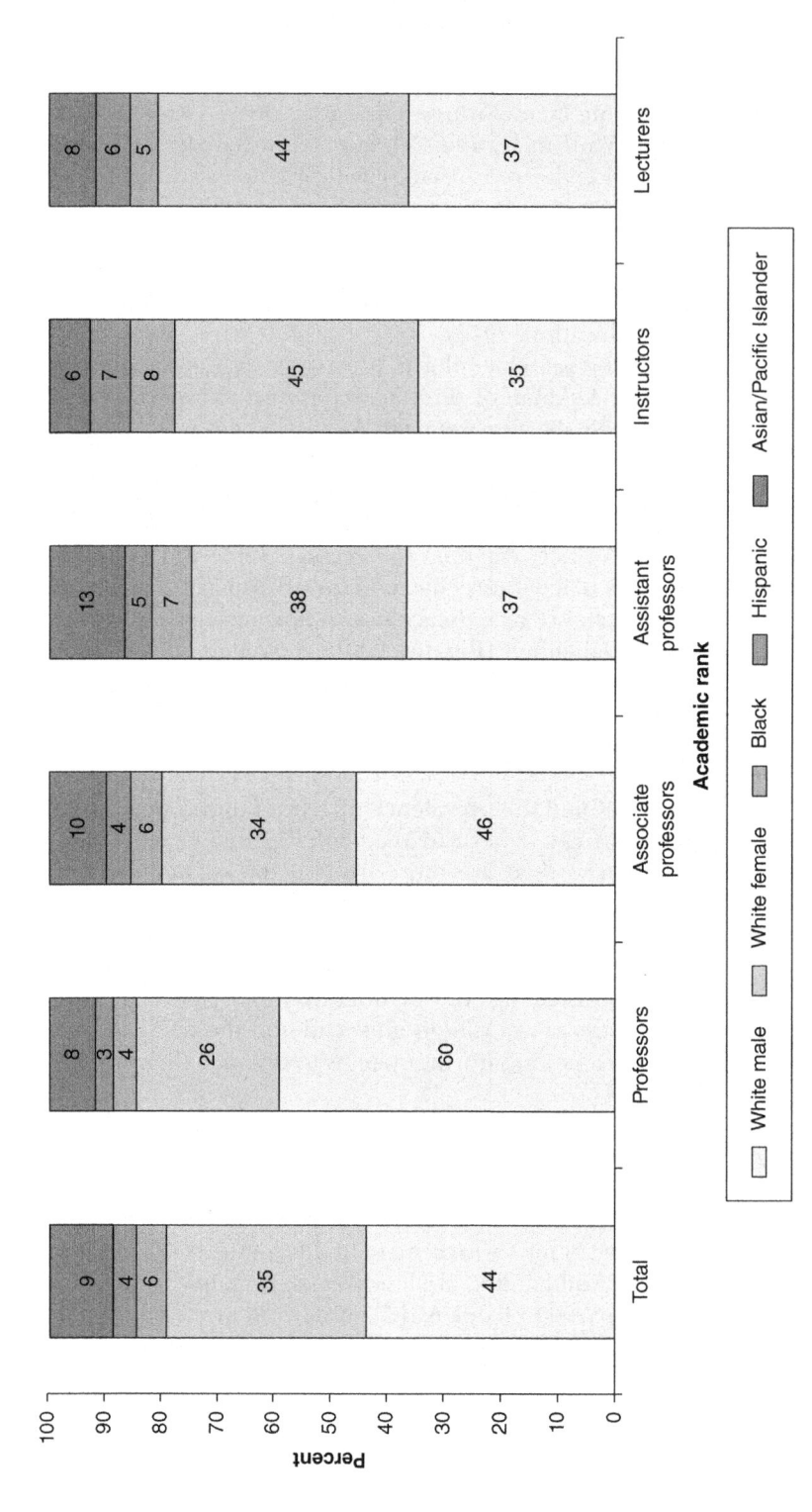

Figure 2.1 Percentage of full-time faculty in postsecondary institutions (USA) whose race/ethnicity was known, by academic rank, selected race/ethnicity and sex: Fall 2011

in higher education institutions (Trix and Psenka, 2003) which involve subjective selection processes that assess whether individuals are 'worthy' of employment (Erickson and Shultz, 1982). Marchant and Newman (1994) suggest that competitive processes in USA higher education are related to conflict between teaching and research agendas which result in a 'publish or perish' attitude. Alger (1998) argues that the processes that exist in gaining tenure often work to disadvantage those from Black African American backgrounds, resulting in job insecurity. Some researchers have suggested that the processes involved in gaining tenure and achieving promotion in USA universities are not based on a fair performance merit system (Lauer, 1991). This may also be evidenced by the greater concentration of Black African American academics in less prestigious institutions, such as those which favour teaching over research (Konrad and Pfeffer, 1991). Jackson suggests that, 'Acknowledging this problem, many institutions of higher education have framed rhetoric around diversifying the higher education workforce, yet few initiatives have resulted in significant outcomes (Jackson, 2008: 1009–1010).

Race and gender continue to play a significant role in recruitment and selection processes (Futoran and Wyer, 1986) in which search committees focus on the subjective perceptions of candidate which are often the result of unconscious bias (Cesare, 1996) from which decisions to appoint are made based on whether a candidates' 'face fits' rather than their experience and qualifications (Zebrowitz et al., 1991). Davison and Burke (2000) in their research found that Black African American females were more likely to be rated lower for their suitability for a post compared to White candidates (Swim and Sanna, 1996). Others (Prewett-Livingston et al., 1996) have suggested that selectors are more likely to rate candidates highly when they are from similar backgrounds to themselves. There is a plethora of research to suggest the prevalence of covert and subtle racist processes that continue to exist in selection processes in universities in the USA; this behaviour is subtle and indirect and is often directed towards those from Black African American backgrounds (Dovidio and Gaertner, 2000). Dovidio and Gaertner refer to this process as one of 'aversive racism' which characterises, 'the racial attitudes of many whites who endorse egalitarian values, who regard themselves as non-prejudiced, but who discriminate in subtle rationalisable ways' (2000: 315).

Jackson (2008) has identified particular processes which disadvantage Black African American academics: lack of adequate support for promotion and gaining tenure, the revolving door syndrome, tokenism, typecasting, one minority per pot, and the brown on brown taboo. Research continues to suggest that the lack of support for Black African American academics needs to be addressed in order to create greater diversity and equality in universities (Smith et al., 1996; Turner and Myers, 2000). Such a lack of support reported by Black and minority staff in higher education institutions is also demonstrated by lack of a commitment to provide financial support for research activities such as conference attendance, '... the need for support from fellow faculty colleagues of colour is one of the most influential factors for the promotion and tenure among faculty of colour' (Jackson, 2008: 1013). Black African American staff are more likely to leave higher educational institutions if they feel discriminated against. This has also been referred to as the 'revolving door syndrome' (Smith, 1994). Bensimon et al. (2000) suggest that the 'revolving door syndrome' is an aspect that has to be considered when decisions about the retention of Black and minority staff are made, particularly concerning aspects of fairness and equity in comparison to how their White colleagues are treated in institutions.

> It is imperative that academic chairpersons figure out ways to minimise the influence of a formerly racially segregated academic community and 'legislated integration'. Although legislation or policy can reduce blatant discrimination and racism on the nation's campuses, it cannot create a community of collegiality among faculty members in a department.
> (Jackson, 2008: 1014)

'Tokenism' refers to Black colleagues being made to feel that they have only been employed by their organisations because they are Black, rather than because they have the experience and qualifications to perform the job well. As a result, Black and minority ethnic colleagues feel they have to constantly prove their worth to their White colleagues and are reminded by their colleagues that they should be grateful to be employed by the institution (Turner and Myers, 2000). 'Predicating the hire of one person of colour builds into the concept of a 'token hire' because this contributes further to the isolation by being 'the one' in the department' (Jackson, 2008: 1014). Tokenism is also displayed by the unequal treatment of Black academics in which they are marginalised and isolated (Jackson, 2001). Jackson (2006) argues that it is important for those in positions of power to explore the development of effective strategies to support rather than hinder those from Black African American backgrounds in which their presence in the academy is not considered 'tokenistic'.

Research also suggests that Black African American academics are 'typecast' in that they are expected to teach courses and serve on committees which are related to diversity and equity (Turner, et al. 1999). There is an assumption that Black African American colleagues should teach such courses, without a realisation that White and other non-Black colleagues may be placed to do so. Black colleagues are often pushed forward to take on these roles, even in cases when they may not wish to do so (Banks, 1984). 'This form of typecasting may adversely affect faculty members of colour who prefer pursuing other areas of research, thus minimising their academic freedom' (Jackson, 2008: 1014). Some institutions have an unwritten quota system based on 'one minority per pot' in which faculties employ an individual from a Black or minority background in order that they can demonstrate they have addressed aspects of diversity and equity (de la Luz Reyes and Halcon, 1988). Turner and Myers (2000) argue that the research carried out by Black and minority ethnic staff is often defined as the 'brown on brown' taboo in which their research is judged to be based on personal experiences, rather than empirical scientific research that is worthy of study.

> White colleagues often see research by faculty of colour on people of colour as unimportant and not valid. It is ironic that 'white on white' research is afforded legitimacy but 'brown on brown' research is questionable and challenged at the same time as many white social scientists are establishing their professional careers as experts on minority issues.
> (Jackson, 2008: 1015)

Tack and Patitu (1992) found that Black academics report criticism from their White colleagues in which their research is constantly challenged.

Jackson (2008) suggests that inequalities in the academic labour market are related to gender disparities based on a 'debasement filter'. The 'debasement filter' refers to a filtering process in which the applications of Black candidates are viewed negatively, in that their experiences are devalued compared to White candidates. Such criteria disadvantage Black African men:

> the results suggest that the hiring practices in the academic workforce could be restructured to minimise the disparate effects on African American men, thereby limiting racial bias in personal decisions and ultimately addressing the resulting race segregation of the higher education workforce.
> (Jackson, 2008: 1024)

Power in the academy?

Significant economic, social and financial changes in the global labour market have affected higher education institutions. Consequently, there is greater pressure on the availability of jobs and job security remains a key aspect in the competition for promotion and progression in higher education. Such pressures have affected job security, working and pay conditions. Some researchers have suggested that in order to address inequality and fragility in higher education, aspects of who has power and how it is used in the academy have to be challenged. Weber and Vandeyar (2008) suggest that,

> Professors wield power. Inside a critical institution of modern society, professors in almost all countries and often over several centuries have

controlled curricula, admissions, have had a decisive say in tertiary governance and institutional culture in so far as it concerns teaching and the production of academic knowledge.

(2008: 176)

In relation to this, Torres and Schugurensky state, 'Professors are increasingly engaged in competitive behaviour similar to the one prevailing in the marketplace. Academics must develop an entrepreneurial approach' (2002: 446). Changes in higher education have led to an increase in student recruitment in which diversity and inclusion will no longer be at the forefront of the equity agenda. Weber and Vandeyar state,

The international trends towards privatisation, massification, entrepreneurialism, research 'outputs' – the McDonaldisation of higher education – has meant that there is less space for the cultural inclusiveness and multiplicity of knowledge celebrated by several scholars in our field of study at the turn of the century.

(2008: 190)

This chapter has explored the different higher educational contexts in the UK and the USA. It has also provided contextual data on how higher education operates in the two different social and political contexts. The chapter has focused on equality policies in the UK and the USA, as well as exploring how Black academics are positioned in higher education in the UK and the USA. The following chapter will outline the methodology used in the research.

Notes

1 http://www.hesa.ac.uk/index.php?option=com_content&task=view&id=3106&Itemid=161.
2 http://www.hesa.ac.uk/content/view/3129/#eth.
3 OFSTED is the Office for Standards in Education, Children's Services and Skills. OFSTED reports directly to parliament to provide independent and impartial assessment of educational services. They inspect and regulate services which care for children and young people and those which provide education and skills for learners of all ages, such as schools and early years providers.
4 http://www.equalityhumanrights.com/advice-and-guidance/public-sector-equality-duty/introduction-to-the-equality-duty/
5 http://www.equalityhumanrights.com/advice-and-guidance/public-sector-equality-duty/introduction-to-the-equality-duty/
6 http://www.equalityhumanrights.com/advice-and-guidance/further-and-higher-education-providers-guidance/public-sector-equality-duties/
7 http://www.athenaswan.org.uk/.
8 http://www.timeshighereducation.co.uk/story.aspx?storyCode=2004766.
9 http://www.timeshighereducation.co.uk/story.aspx?storyCode=2004766.
10 http://www.ecu.ac.uk/our-projects/gender-equality-charter-mark-consultation-and-development.

11 http://www.ecu.ac.uk/our-projects/race-equality-charter-mark.
12 Black African American is the term that is commonly used in the USA to refer to those whose ancestors originated from Africa.
13 http://nces.ed.gov/programs/digest/d12/.
14 http://nces.ed.gov/programs/digest/d12/.

References

Acker, S. and Feuerverger, G. (1996) Doing good and feeling bad: The work of women university teachers. *Cambridge Journal of Education.* 26, pp.401–422.

Adeleye-Fayemi, B. (2004) Creating and sustaining feminist space in Africa: Local and global challenges in the twenty-first century. In Ricciutelli, L., Miles, A. and McFadden, S. (eds) *Feminist Politics, Activism and Vision.* Toronto: Inanda Publications, pp.100–111.

Ahmed, S. (2007) 'You end up doing the document rather than doing the doing': Diversity, race equality and the politics of documentation. *Race, Ethnicity and Education.* 30 (4), pp.590–609.

Alger, J. (1998) Minority faculty and measuring merit: Start by playing fair. *Academe.* 84, p.71.

Allen, W., Epps, E., Guillory, A., Suh, S. and Bonous-Hammarth, M. (2000) The Black academic: Faculty status among African Americans in US higher education. *Journal of Negro Education.* 69 (1–2), pp.112–127.

Banks, W. (1984) Afro-American scholars in the university: Roles and conflicts. *American Behavioural Scientist.* 27, pp.325–338.

Bassanini, A. and Saint-Martin, A. (2008) *The Price of Prejudice: Labour market discrimination on the grounds of race and ethnicity.* London: OECD Employment Outlook.

Beattie, G. and Johnson, P. (2011) Unconscious bias in recruitment and promotion and the need to promote equality. *Perspectives: Policy and Practice in Higher Education.* 16, pp.7–13.

Bensimon, E., Ward, K. and Sanders, K. (2000) *The Department Chair's Role in Developing New Faculty into Teachers and Scholars.* Bolton, MA: Anker.

Bertrand, M. and Mullainathan, S. (2004) Are Emily and Greg more employable than Lakisha and Jamal? A field experiment on labour market discrimination. *American Economic Review.* 94 (4), pp.991–1013.

Bhopal, K. (2014) *The Experience of BME Leaders in Higher Education: Aspirations in the face of inequality.* London: Leadership Foundation for Higher Education Stimulus Paper.

Bhopal, K. and Jackson, J. (2013) *The Experiences of Black and Minority Ethnic Academics: Multiple identities and career progression.* Southampton: EPSRC.

Breakwell, G. and Tytherleigh, M. (2008) *The Characteristics, Roles and Selection of Vice-Chancellors. Final Report.* London: Leadership Foundation for Higher Education.

Cesare, S. (1996) Subjective judgment and selection interview: A methodological review. *Public Personnel Management.* 25, pp.291–306.

Clark, K. and Drinkwater, S. (2007) *Ethnic minorities in the labour market: Dynamics and diversity.* London: Joseph Rowntree Foundation.

Collins, P. (1990) *Black Feminist Thought: Knowledge, consciousness, and the politics of empowerment.* Boston, MA: Unwin Hyman.

Crofts, M. and Pilkington, A. (2012) *The Politics of Equality and Diversity in Higher Education*. Paper presented to: Fifth Equality, Diversity and Inclusion International Conference 2012, Toulouse, France, 23–26 July 2012.

Davison, K. and Burke, M. (2000) Sex discrimination in simulated selection contexts: A meta-analytic study. *Journal of Vocational Behaviour.* 56, pp.225–248.

De la Luz Reyes, M. and Halcon, J. (1988) Racism in academia: The old wolf revisited. *Harvard Educational Review.* 58, pp.299–314.

Dearing Report, The (1997) *Higher Education in the Learning Society.* London: HMSO.

Deem, R., Morley, L. and Tlili, A. (2005) *Negotiating Equity in HEIs: A case-study analysis of policies and staff experiences.* London: Higher Education Funding Council for England.

Dixson, A. and Rousseau, K. (2005) And we are still not saved: Critical Race Theory in education ten years later. *Race, Ethnicity and Education.* 8 (1), pp.7–27.

Dovidio, J. and Gaertner, S. (2000) Aversive Racism and Selection Decisions. *Psychological Science.* 11 (4), pp.315–319.

Education Reform Act 1988. London: HMSO.

Elevation Networks Trust (2012) *Race to the Top: The experience of black students in higher education.* London: Elevation Networks Trust.

Equality Challenge Unit (2011) *The Experience of Black and Minority Ethnic Staff in Higher Education in England.* London: ECU.

Equality Charter Marks (2013) *Frequently Asked Questions.* London: ECU. Equality Act 2010. London: HMSO.

Erickson, F. and Shultz, J. (1982) *The Counsellor as Gatekeeper: Social interaction in interviews.* New York: Academic Press.

Fredman, S. (2001) Combating racism with human rights: The right to equality. In Fredman, S. (ed) *Discrimination and Human Rights: The case of racism.* Oxford: Oxford University Press, pp.11–20.

Further and Higher Education Act 1992. London: HMSO.

Futoran, G. and Wyer, R. (1986) The effects of traits and gender stereotypes on occupational suitability judgments and the recall for judgment-relevant information. *Journal of Experimental Social Psychology.* 22, pp.475–503.

Green, D., Erdos, G. and Shahi, A. (2000) *Institutional Racism and the Police: Fact or fiction?* Wiltshire: Institute for the Study of Civil Society.

Gregory, S. (2006) The cultural constructs of race, gender and class: A study of how Afro-Caribbean women academics negotiate their careers. *International Journal of Qualitative Studies in Education.* 1 (3), pp.347–366.

Gwele, N. (2002) Racial relations in selected faculties in English language historically white universities in South Africa. *Society in Transformation.* 33, pp.134–151.

Henry, F., Choi, A. and Kobayashi, A. (2013) *The Representation of Racialised Faculty at Selected Canadian Universities.* Canada: Comparative Education Services.

HESA (2014) http://www.hesa.ac.uk/content/view/3129/#eth [Accessed 20 June 2014].

Hey, V. (2011) Affective asymmetries: Academics, austerity and the mis/recognition of emotion. *Contemporary Social Science*, Special Issue, Challenge, Change or Crisis in Higher Education? 6 (2), pp.207–222.

Hey, V., Dunne, M. and Aynsley, S. (2011) *The Experience of Black and Minority Ethnic Staff in Higher Education in England.* Project Report. London: Equality Challenge Unit.

House of Commons Business, Innovation and Skills Committee (2013) *Inquiry into the Future of Higher Education, Evidence from the Russell Group of Universities*. London: House of Commons.

Jackson, J. F. L. (2001) A new test for diversity: Retaining African American administrators at predominantly White institutions. In Jones, L. (ed) *Retaining African Americans in Higher Education: Challenging paradigms for retaining students, faculty, and administrators*. Sterling, VA: Stylus, pp.93–101.

Jackson, J. F. L. (2006) Hiring practices of African American males in academic leadership positions at American colleges and universities: An employment trends and disparate impact analysis. *Teachers College Record*. 108, pp.316–338.

Jackson, J. F. L. (2008) Race segregation across the academic workforce: Factors that may contribute to the disparate representation of African American men. *American Behavioural Scientist*. 51, pp.1004–1029.

Jawitz, J. (2012) Race and assessment practice in South Africa. *Race, Ethnicity and Education*. 15(4), pp.545–559.

Kandola, B. (2009) *The Value of Difference: Eliminating bias in organisations*. Oxford: Pearn Kandola.

Kaplin, W. and Lee, B. (1995) *The Law of Higher Education*. San Francisco, CA: Jossey-Bass.

Konrad, A. and Pfeffer, J. (1991) Understanding the hiring of women and minorities in educational institutions. *Sociology of Education*. 64, pp.141–157.

Lauer, A. (1991) Searching for answers: Should universities create merit pay systems? *NACUBO Business Officer*, pp.52–54.

Law, I., Phillips, D. and Turney, L. (2004) *Institutional Racism in Higher Education*. Stoke on Trent: Trentham.

Lefranc, A. (2010) Unequal opportunities and ethnic origin: The labour market outcomes of second generation immigrants in France. *American Behavioural Scientist*. 53, pp.1851–1882.

Lewis, K., Hammond, J. and Horvers, K. (2012) In challenging times, might the Equality Act 2010 assist universities in embracing and embedding widening participation? *Perspectives: Policy and Practice in Higher Education*. 16 (1), pp.19–22. http://www.tandfonline.com/doi/ref/10.1080/13603108.2011.611830#.VQcRIikwj8t [Accessed 16 March 2015].

Li, Y. and Heath, A. (2009) Struggling onto the ladder, climbing up the rungs: Employment status and class position by minority ethnic groups in Britain (1972–2005). In Stillwell, J., Norman, P,. Thomas, C. and Surridge. P. (eds) *Population, Employment, Health and Well-being*. Dordrecht: Springer, pp.83–97.

Lumby, J. (2012) *What Do We Know about Leadership in Higher Education?* London: Leadership Foundation for Higher Education.

Lymperopoulou, K. and Parameshwaran, M. (2014) *How are Ethnic Inequalities in Education Changing?* University of Manchester: Centre for Dynamics of Ethnicity.

Marchant, G. and Newman, I. (1994) Faculty activities and rewards: Views from education administrators in the USA. *Assessment and Evaluation in Higher Education*. 9 (2), pp.145–152.

National Equality Panel (2010) *An Anatomy of Inequality in the UK*. London: NEP.

Niemann, Y. and Dovidio, J. (1998) Relationship of solo status, academic rank, and perceived distinctiveness to job satisfaction of racial/ethnic minorities. *Journal of Applied Psychology*. 83 (1), pp.55–71.

Office for National Statistics (2013) Percentage of graduates working in non graduate jobs. http://www.ons.gov.uk/ons/rel/lmac/graduates-in-the-labour-market/2013/sty-graduates-in-the-labour-market.html [Accessed 16 March 2015].

Okolo, R. and Eddy, J. (1994) A job satisfaction study of faculty at historically black colleges and universities in Texas. *College Student Journal.* 28 (3), pp.345–346.

O'Leary, J. (2013) Advancing access and admissions. Report from The Sutton Trust Summit, November 2013. London: The Sutton Trust.

Olsen, D., Maple, S. and Stage, F. (1995) Women and minority faculty job satisfaction. *Journal of Higher Education.* 66 (3), pp.267–293.

Pager, D., Western, B. and Bonikowski, B. (2009) Discrimination in a low wage labour market: A field experiment. *American Sociological Review.* 74, pp.777–799.

Pilkington, A. (2013) The interacting dynamics of institutional racism in higher education. *Race, Ethnicity and Education.* 16 (2), pp.225–245.

Prewett-Livingston, A., Field, H., Veres, J. and Lewis, P. (1996) Effects of race on interview ratings in a situational panel interview. *Journal of Applied Psychology.* 81, pp.178–186.

Race Relations (Amendment) Act 2000. London: HMSO.

Richardson, J. (2010) Widening participation without widening attainment: The case of ethnic minority students. *Psychology Teaching Review.* 16(1), pp.37–45.

Riggins, S. (2001) *The Language and Politics of Exclusion.* Oxford: Blackwell.

Rooth, D. (2010) Automatic associations and discrimination in hiring: Real world evidence. *Labour Economics.* 17 (3), pp.523–534.

Ruebain, D. (2012) Aren't we there yet? Why re invigorating the equality agenda is an institutional priority. *Perspectives: Policy and Practice in Higher Education.* 16 (1), pp.3–6.

Schulze, S. (2005) *Academic Research at a South African Higher Education Institution: Quality issues.* South Africa: Department of Further Teacher Education.

Senior, O. (1990) *Working Miracles: Women's lives in the English speaking Caribbean.* Barbados: Cave Hill.

Shiner, M. and Modood, T. (2002) Help or hindrance? Higher education and the route to ethnic equality. *British Journal of Sociology of Education.* 23 (2), pp.209–232.

Simpson, L., Purdam, K., Tajar, A., Fieldhouse, E., Gavalas, V., Tranmer, M., Pritchard, J. and Dorling, D. (2006) *Ethnic Minority Populations and the Labour Market: An analysis of the 1991 and 2001 census.* London: Department of Work and Pensions.

Singh, G. (2009) *Black and Minority Ethnic Students' Participation in Higher Education: Improving retention and success.* York: Higher Education Academy.

Singh, K., Robinson, A. and Williams-Green, J. (1995) Differences in perceptions of African American women and men faculty and administrators. *The Journal of Negro Education.* 64 (4), pp.401–408.

Smith, D., Wolf, L. and Busenberg, B. (1996) *Achieving Faculty Diversity: Debunking the myths.* Washington, DC: Association of American Colleges and Universities.

Smith, R. (1994) Successful recruitment of minority faculty: Commitment, culture, choice. *Journal of the Association for Communication Administration.* 3, pp.152–156.

Snowden, G. (2012) Graduates: Is a 2:1 the best qualification for landing a job? *The Guardian.* 10 February. Available from: http://www.guardian.co.uk/money/2012/feb/10/graduates-best-qualification-landing-job?newsfeed [Accessed 14 May 2014].

Son Hing, L., Greg. S., Chun, Y., Leah, M., Hamilton., P. and Zanna, P. (2008) A two dimensional model that employs explicit and implicit attitudes to characterise prejudice. *Journal of Personality and Social Psychology.* 94, pp.971–987.

Steward, R., Patterson, P., Morales, P., Bartell, P., Dinas, S. and Powers, R. (1995) Women in higher education and job satisfaction: Does interpersonal style matter? *NASPA Journal.* 35 (1), pp.45–53.

Sutton Trust (2011) *Degrees of Success.* London: Sutton Trust.

Swim, J. and Sanna, L. (1996) He's skilled, she's lucky: A meta-analysis of observers' attributions for women's and men's successes and failures. *Personality and Social Psychology Bulletin.* 22, pp.507–519.

Tack, M. and Patitu, C. (1992) *Faculty Job Satisfaction: Women and minorities in peril.* Washington, DC: Higher Education Report No. 4.

Tang, T. and Talpade, M. (1999) Sex differences in satisfaction with pay and co-workers: Faculty and staff at a public institution of higher education. *Public Personnel Management.* 28 (3), pp.345–349.

Tierney, W. (1993) *Building Communities of Difference: Higher education in the twenty-first century.* Westport, CT: Bergin & Garvey.

Times Higher Education (2012) Average salary of full-time academic staff, 2011/12.

Times Higher Education (2013) Twenty% rise in 0.2 contracts. 26 Sept 2013.

Tobias, M., Bhattachrya, A. and White P. (2008) Cross classification of the New Zealand population by ethnicity and deprivation: Trends from 1996 to 2006. *Australian and New Zealand Journal of Public Health.* 32, pp.431–436.

Tolich, M. (2002) Pakeha 'paralysis': Cultural safety for those researching the general population of Aotearoa. *Social Policy Journal of New Zealand.* 19, pp.164–178.

Torres, C. and Schugurensky, D. (2002) The political economy of higher education in the era of neoliberal globalization: Latin America in comparative perspective. *Higher Education.* 43 (4), pp.429–455.

Trix, F. and Psenka, C. (2003) Exploring the colour of glass: Letters of recommendation for female and male medical faculty. *Discourse & Society.* 14, pp.191–220.

Turner, C. and Myers, S. (2000) *Faculty of Color in Academe: Bittersweet success.* Boston: Allyn & Bacon.

Turner, T., Myers, C. and Creswell, J. (1999) Exploring underrepresentation: The case of faculty of color in the Midwest. *Journal of Higher Education.* 70, pp.27–59.

University and College Union (2012) *The Position of Women and BME Staff in Professorial Roles in UK HEIs.* London: UCU.

U.S. Department of Education, National Center for Education Statistics (2012). *The Condition of Education 2012* (NCES 2012-045), Indicator 47.

U.S. Department of Education, National Center for Education Statistics (2013). *The Condition of Education 2013* (NCES 2013-037), Characteristics of Postsecondary Faculty.

Wane, N. (2009) Black Canadian feminist thought: perspectives on equity and diversity in the academy. *Race, Ethnicity and Education.* 12 (1), pp.65–77.

Weber, E. and Vandeyar, V. (2008) A site of struggle: Black academics at historically white universities in South Africa. *Africa Education Review.* 1 (2), pp.175–192.

Williams, B. and Williams, S. (2006) Perceptions of African American male junior faculty on promotion and tenure: Implications for community building and social capital. *Teachers College Record.* 108, pp.287–315.

Yosso, T. (2005) Whose culture has capital? A critical race theory discussion of community cultural wealth. *Race Ethnicity and Education.* 8 (1), pp.69–91.

YouGov poll (2011) *UK Polling Report*. London: YouGov.

Zebrowitz, L., Tenenbaum, D. and Goldstein, L. (1991) The impact of job applicants' facial maturity, gender, and academic achievement on hiring recommendations. *Journal of Applied Social Psychology*. 21, pp.525–548.

Web references

http://www.athenaswan.org.uk/ [Accessed 20 June 2014].

http://www.ecu.ac.uk/our-projects/race-equality-charter-mark. [Accessed 20 May 2014].

http://www.equalityhumanrights.com/advice-and-guidance/public-sector-equality-duty/introduction-to-the-equality-duty/ [Accessed 20 May 2014].

http://www.ecu.ac.uk/our-projects/gender-equality-charter-mark-consultation-and-development [Accessed 20 June 2014].

http://www.hesa.ac.uk/content/view/3129/#eth [Accessed 20 June 2014].

http://nces.ed.gov/programs/digest/d21/ [Accessed 20 May 2014].

http://www.ons.gov.uk/ons/rel/lmac/graduates-in-the-labour-market/2013/sty-graduates-in-the-labour-market.html [Accessed 16 March 2015].

http://www.timeshighereducation.co.uk/story.aspx?storyCode=2004766) [Accessed 20 May 2014].

3 The research and methodology

This book draws upon empirical research conducted in the UK and the USA and is based on a two year study which examined the experiences of BME academics in the academy, particularly in relation to their career progression and career trajectories. This chapter will outline the methodology. The main aims of the study were:

1. To explore the experiences of BME academics in relation to how they were positioned in the academy;
2. To examine the use and existence of support and mentoring networks;
3. To analyse aspects of career promotion and progression; and
4. To investigate experiences of exclusion and marginalisation in higher education institutions.

Respondents participated in in-depth semi-structured interviews. Interview questions focused on: experiences of becoming an academic and entering the academy; promotion and progression; career development; how respondents viewed their roles in the academy and how their identities were affected by this; the process of the REF; the impact of financial cuts in higher education institutions and the effects of this on individual career trajectories and the existence and effectiveness of support structures.

The study

Sixty-five respondents participated in the study; thirty-five respondents were working in universities in the UK and thirty were working in universities in the USA. Respondents participated in in-depth semi-structured qualitative interviews; these were either face to face, Skype interviews or via the telephone. Participants were asked to sign a consent form to participate and were informed that they could withdraw from the study at any time without explanation. None of the respondents took this option and many reported that they were glad to participate in the study to speak about their experiences in the academy. All of the respondents were given the opportunity to read their transcripts, only a minority did so and none of the respondents objected to their responses being used in dissemination or publication purposes. The majority of respondents were very positive about the research and wanted to share their experiences, particularly emphasising that they wanted their voices to be heard.

> I just wanted to thank you for giving me the chance to talk about these issues. Quite often, these issues that we have spoken about become silenced in faculties and only happen behind closed doors and sometimes in corridors. It is the chairs of departments that have to recognise that these things need to be spoken about at their place of work and not only in a research project (USA respondent).

> One has to be careful when speaking about issues to do with race – because there is a fear that it might be held against you – and as Black male, I could be seen as someone who is always talking about race and so has a problem. This opportunity to share my experiences in a safe and relaxed environment is something I am grateful for – it also shows me that this kind of research is very important and needs to be done and also disseminated widely so that all academics know some of the issues that need to be addressed in universities (UK respondent).

> I have enjoyed speaking to you about my experiences, these are issues that are rarely discussed and should be discussed more in my opinion. It is important that these issues are brought to the fore so that all academics know what is really going in the academy (UK respondent).

The following sections will outline the background information of respondents who participated in the study.

UK respondents

Thirty-five respondents who were working in universities in the UK participated in the study. Respondents represented a diverse range of backgrounds in terms of their gender, age, academic roles and the types of universities they were employed in. The tables below provide detailed background information on respondents who participated in the study.

Table 3.1 Gender and employment level of respondents (UK)

	Professor	Senior lecturer	Lecturer	Senior research assistant	Research assistant	Total
Female	4	5	6	2	1	18
Male	3	5	5	2	2	17
Total	7	10	11	4	3	35

Table 3.2 Ethnic background of respondents (UK)

	Black British	Black African	Indian	Pakistani	Bangladeshi	Mixed White/Black	Mixed White/Asian
Male	4	4	1	2	0	1	0
Female	7	6	3	3	0	2	2
Total	11	10	4	5	0	3	2

Two male senior research assistants and all research assistants were on temporary contracts, all other respondents were on permanent contracts. One female lecturer had just come to the end of her fixed term contract and was in the process of applying for a new job. Eleven respondents were working in Russell Group universities (at senior lecturer or lecturer grades); all others were working in 'new' (post-1992) universities. The age range of respondents varied from 25 to 58. The majority of respondents had worked for more than five years in higher education institutions, with the exception of six who had completed their doctorates in the previous two years. Respondents participated in in-depth semi-structured interviews. Twenty-two of the in-depth interviews were face to face, ten were telephone interviews and three were conducted via Skype. All of the interviews were digitally recorded and the data transcribed.

US respondents

Thirty respondents working in universities in the USA participated in the study. All but two of the respondents defined themselves as 'Black African American' (a term used by the respondents themselves). One academic defined herself as Indian. Her parents were of Indian origin and moved to the USA from the UK fifteen years ago. She had been working in her current university for three years. Another respondent defined herself as Latina and had been working in her current university for six years. All of the respondents were working in public universities: some were working in prestigious research intensive universities (12) and others were working in universities that were teaching led. The following table provides background details for respondents working in universities in the USA.

Table 3.3 Gender and employment level of respondents (USA)

	Full Professor	Associate Professor	Assistant Professor	Teaching Assistant	PhD Student	Total
Female	6	4	3	1	1	15
Male	7	4	4	0	0	15
Total	13	8	7	1	1	30

Thirteen of the respondents working in universities in the USA were full professors (one of whom was a 'distinguished professor'). All of the full professors had tenured positions and six of the associate professors were considering applying for their tenured positions in the next three to five years. Fifteen of the interviews were face to face, five were conducted over the telephone and ten were conducted via Skype.

Telephone interviews

A number of interviews were conducted via the telephone due to the large distances between respondents who were working in universities in the USA and the author who was based in the UK. Conducting an interview via telephone can have different effects on the interview process compared to face to face interviews (Frey, 1989). The interview questions have to be clear and focused due to the absence of non-verbal and physical cues. Telephone interviews cannot be as long in duration as face to face interviews due to the absence of these cues. Telephone interviews, however, can offer several advantages: they are cheap and easy; they can reduce bias in terms of gender, race and ethnicity; and they can offer greater anonymity compared to face to face interviews. Some disadvantages include: a difficulty in controlling the interview fully; a high refusal rate; and limited access to the target population in cases where individuals may not have access to a telephone (Benini, 2000).

Telephone interviews are considered more effective for the gathering of quantitative survey data rather than qualitative ethnographic methods (Aday, 1996). There has been little research which has explored the use of telephone interviews for qualitative methods (Sturges and Hanrahan, 2002; Sweet, 2004), and there is evidence to suggest that the use of telephone interviews promotes greater communication between the researcher and the respondent in which rich and detailed data is obtained. They are also considered cheap, safe and can reach those who are located in remote geographical areas (Sweet, 2002). However, disadvantages include the absence of visual cues, respondents becoming distracted from the main questions and the fact that telephone interviews must be shorter than face to face interviews so fewer topics will be covered during the interview (Creswell, 1998). The absence of visual cues can influence the interview due to a lack of contextual information and consequently there is less likelihood of opportunities to probe respondents; as well as a possible misinterpretation of responses (Sturges and Hanrahan, 2004). Others, however, have argued that respondents may feel more relaxed and willing to discuss private and sensitive information with researchers when they are not face to face with the interviewer. Consequently, respondents will feel confident to discuss detailed and personal aspects of their lives (Chapple, 1999).

Skype interviews

The use of Skype as an online tool to conduct interviews has increasingly become popular, particularly due to the availability of cheap online technology. Skype is a piece of online software which provides several different types of communications for users. The most popular type of communication for conducting research is the use of video from which researchers can conduct face to face online interviews. As a relatively new phenomenon, there has been little research which explored the use of Skype as a research tool for conducting research (Booth, 2008; Kazmer and Xie, 2008). Samure and Given[1] suggest several advantages of the method: it is user friendly, inexpensive and allows interviews to be conducted over a wide geographical area. Disadvantages include: time lags in conversation, and the potential for loss of signal which can affect the flow of the interview. Skype interviews were used for this study as it enabled interviews to be conducted in different geographical locations (such as from the UK to the USA), covering vast areas without the researcher having to travel long distances. Consequently a cross cultural study was conducted at a low cost and low inconvenience for the researcher. Some researchers (Hine, 2004) have identified the benefits of using Skype as a research tool: 'a style of ethnography that involves real-time engagement with the field and multiple ways of interacting with informants has proved key in highlighting the processes through which online interaction becomes socially meaningful to participants' (Hine, 2004: 27). Dujardin (2009) has argued that the use of Skype for online interviews enables researchers to engage with 'key informants' in a detailed way. Others have suggested that the existence of two different environments of online interviews are advantageous; synchronous environments (such as real chat rooms and instant messenger communications) which provide the researcher and respondent with a forum that is similar to face to face interviews in which questions can be asked back and forth between the two participants; and asynchronous environments which are based on the use of emails and message boards which are often used in survey research (Berg, 2007: 112). However, Fontana and Frey (2008) suggest that online interviewing is often impossible to do well. Others have argued, however, that online surveys are extremely useful when conducting quantitative research (Schaefer and Dillman, 1998).

Different ethical issues have to be considered when using online research instruments (Markham, 2008). Markham (2008) points out that some internet communication which is perceived by the researcher and respondent as being private may in fact be accessible by others who are not involved in the research project. Researchers should be aware of these issues and, if this is the case, respondents should be informed of this before they agree to participate in the research. Consequently such research would raise questions of anonymity and confidentiality. Informed consent may also be difficult to obtain in writing if the participant wishes to remain anonymous throughout the research (Markham, 2008). Sullivan (2012: 960) argues that,

Through the use of communication programs, our reach is potentially limitless, at least geographically, for interviewwing depending on the topic of interest. We are not only able to communicate verbally with those all around the world, but we can actually interact visually using video recording devices in real-time, allowing for at least a mimicked face-to-face interaction.

Bertrand and Bourdeau suggest that:

> a Skype to Skype research interview is more than a face to face research interview. In fact, recorded audio and video data could be more studied exactly with the same material. The recorded interview is a mirror of what it was in reality. Non-verbal data are visible and don't depend on the interview's spare notes nor his memories.
>
> (2010: 73)

Whilst there are advantages and disadvantages to using both types of interviews, Skype interviews were used for convenience and ease of access to respondents, and where possible, face to face interviews were conducted with respondents.

Sample

In the UK, employment data for universities is collected on the ethnicity of employees, but such data is confidential. When universities were contacted to provide information on the ethnic background of their employees, they declined to give such information and responded that the information was confidential and only for the use of individual organisations. A similar process was followed in the USA: universities were contacted to provide data regarding the ethnic background of respondents but such data was not publicly available. Even though such data is collected for specific employment monitoring processes, universities do not disclose such information as it is confidential.

Consequently, respondents were contacted via personal contacts and a snowball sample. Respondents were asked if they wanted to participate and if they knew of other BME academics who may want to participate in the study. I also used my own personal networks and contacts to make links with BME academics, such as special interest groups on race, ethnicity and education, and other education networks. I am aware of the diverse range of problems associated with snowball sampling and the possibility of bias in favour of respondents who are eager to discuss their experiences and the implications this may have on the research process and the research relationship between myself and respondents. However, snowball sampling is often used to study groups that are either difficult to identify or, 'hard to reach'. Sarantakos states,

This method is employed when the lack of sampling frames makes it impossible for the researcher to achieve a probability sample, when the target population is unknown, or when it is difficult to approach the respondents in any other way. In many cases, snowball sampling is the only way of securing a sample for the study.

(Sarantakos, 2005: 166)

The problem with using snowball sampling as a technique is that it can build in 'security' (Lee, 1993) because the contacts may be well known and trusted by each other. However, this may lead to bias in the selection process particularly as relationships between the participants in the sample may consist of 'reciprocity and transitivity' (Lee, 1993: 67). It may be possible for example that respondents have knowledge of each other and are engaged in relationships which could affect the research responses and the homogeneity of the sample. As a result, snowball sampling could alter the research so that it becomes a convenience sample which may compromise generalisability. However, in some cases the use of snowball sampling may be the only method of selecting respondents, particularly if the research is sensitive and involves 'hard to reach' groups.

Ethical issues

Ethical issues are considered to be significantly important when conducting research with individuals. Codes of ethics focus on physical or mental harm to respondents, the use of covert research, issues of anonymity and confidentiality as well as the invasion of privacy and deception (Pfeifer, 2000). Generally, most researchers consider four aspects of ethics in research: professional standards and ethical conduct, the researcher-respondent relationship, the researcher–researcher relationship, and the treatment of animals in research (Bailey, 1988; Sproull, 1988). Professional standards and ethical conduct include aspects such as maintaining objectivity in the conduct of social research, upholding professional integrity, and demonstrating responsibility in the research process as well as reporting data accurately (Sarantakos, 2005). The researcher–respondent relationship includes: treating respondents respectfully, for instance, not giving respondents false impressions; providing respondents with clear information on the types of questions they will be asked; and ensuring a right to privacy and confidentiality and informed consent (Sproull, 1988).

The researcher–respondent relationship is also based on the correct use of data obtained for research purposes; for example Sarantakos states, 'Inappropriate use of data belonging to other researchers in a report is unethical and constitutes malpractice' (2005: 21). This includes: misleading ascription of authorship, misuse of authority and role, and plagiarism (Sarantakos, 2005). Researchers are expected to adhere to such aspects of professional standards.

50 *The research and methodology*

Lichtman (2010) identifies two kinds of privacy in the protection of respondents' anonymity; institutional and individual. The researcher has to be careful to protect the identity of the respondent and their organisation; if either is revealed this could cause some difficulties for those involved in the research. Lichtman states,

> Any individual participating in a research study has a reasonable expectation that privacy will be guaranteed. Consequently, no identifying information about the individual should be revealed in written or verbal communication form. Further, any group or organisation participating in a research study has reasonable expectation that its identity will not be revealed.
> (Lichtman, 2010: 54)

For this study, respondents signed a consent form and a participant information sheet detailing the aims and objectives of the study. They were also informed that they could withdraw from the study at any time without explanation. Respondents were also given the opportunity to see the interview transcripts and to change them if they wished; none of the respondents decided to do this. Ethical guidelines from the British Educational Research Association were followed and ethical clearance was obtained from the host university. Whilst the respondents spoke about their own personal experiences, I was able to control how much information I would use for dissemination purposes. I discussed with respondents (so that it was clear from the outset) that if any quotes and information were used, I would ensure that the respondent or their institution would not be identified. All of the respondents agreed for their quotes to be used for dissemination purposes. The following section will outline the data analysis process.

Data analysis

The data was analysed using methods of grounded theory as developed by Charmaz (2006). Data was explored by examining the different themes and concepts that respondents spoke about in their responses. The codes were grouped into concepts in order to generate meaning from the concepts and categories were formed which determined the creation of a theoretical understanding of the data. Glaser and Strauss (1967) first introduced the concept of grounded theory to refer to ways of analysing data in which theory emerges from the data. Grounded theory includes the use of theoretical sampling and specific types of coding which includes open coding, axial coding and selective coding (Strauss and Corbin, 1990). Davidson suggests that,

> Open coding is based on the concept of data being cracked open as a means of identifying relevant categories. Axial coding is most often used when categories are in an advanced stage of development and

selective category is used when the 'core category' or central category that correlates all other categories in the theory, is identified and related to other categories.

(Davidson, 2002: 4)

Charmaz (2006) developed the main principles of grounded theory through the gathering of rich data, the process of coding during the development of the analysis, and memo writing to contribute to the development and further analysis of the codes. Charmaz also emphasises how theoretical sampling can contribute to the analysis and coding of the data during a selective process that is constantly refined whilst addressing the main categories of analysis as they emerge. The development of theory is based on the different stages in which ideas and analysis emerge through the data whilst the coding is taking place. As a result of this process, grounded theory enables the researcher to construct an original theory based on the interpretation of the data.

> Our grounded theory adventure starts as we enter the field where we gather data. We step forward from our disciplinary perspectives with a few tools and provisional concepts. A grounded theory journey may take several varied routes, depending on where we want to go and where our analysis takes us.
>
> (Charmaz, 2006: 13)

Grounded theory is particularly suited to ethnographic methods. Whilst there are different types of ethnographic methods that could have been used for this study, it was the in-depth interview that was considered the most appropriate. For the purposes of this research study, interviews were considered as directed conversations or conversations with a purpose (Lofland and Lofland, 1995):

> Intensive interviewing permits an in-depth exploration of a particular topic or experience and thus, is a useful method for interpretive enquiry... the in-depth nature of an intensive interview fosters eliciting each participant's interpretation of his or her experience. The interviewer seeks to understand the topic and the interview participant has the relevant experiences to shed light on it.
>
> (Charmaz, 2006: 25, see also Fontana and Frey, 1994)

Charmaz (2006) suggests that if a researcher decides to use grounded theory, the interview should be devised around broad, open ended questions in order that the interview questions can focus on particular aspects the researcher is interested in. 'The combination of how you construct the questions and conduct the interview shapes how well you achieve a balance between making the interview open ended and focussing on significant statements' (Charmaz,

2006: 26). The structure of the interview can vary from what is considered a 'loosely guided exploration of topics to semi-structured focussed questions. Although the intensive interview may be conversational, it follows a different etiquette' (Charmaz, 2006: 26). It is crucial to understand the data so that analysis can take place. This can take time, but 'studying your data prompts you to learn nuances of your research participants' language and meaning' (Charmaz, 2006: 34).

The coding process in using grounded theory is crucial: 'Coding means categorising segments of data with a short name that simultaneously summarises and accounts for each piece of data. Your codes show how you select, separate and sort data to begin an analytic accounting of them' (Charmaz, 2006: 43). From this understanding the data was analysed around particular themes which were used to generate information to provide the basis of a conceptual and theoretical understanding of the key issues that respondents spoke about. 'Coding is the pivotal link between collecting data and developing an emergent theory to explain these data. Through coding, you *define* what is happening in the data and begin to grapple with what it means' (Charmaz, 2006: 46, original emphasis). For the purposes of this study, the use of grounded theory as a data analysis method was the most appropriate and provided the basis of a theoretical foundation for the data analysis to take place.

Identity and positionality in the research process

All of the interviews in the USA were conducted by the author and the interviews in the UK were conducted by the author and a research assistant who was from an Asian Indian background. When the interviews were conducted via telephone, both researchers were asked about their ethnic identity. Some (though not all) of the respondents said they felt more comfortable speaking to a minority ethnic researcher about their experiences of working in the academy, particularly issues relating to racism, exclusion and marginalisation, than if they were speaking to a White researcher. My own experience of conducting interviews with respondents was overwhelmingly positive. I conducted all of the interviews with respondents working in the USA and a majority of those with UK respondents. On almost all occasions I was asked about my own ethnic identity and my own position in the academy. I was also on several occasions asked about my own experiences of racism and exclusion and in a minority of cases I was asked to describe these in detail. Research suggests that when respondents are able to share their experiences with the researcher, greater trust leads to openness and empathy in the interview process (see Bhopal, 2010). The more I revealed about my own personal experiences of exclusion and marginalisation, the more respondents were willing to open up and reveal their experiences. The majority of respondents were grateful that they were able to voice their views of their experiences in their universities and none of the respondents expressed concern about whether their responses would impact upon their careers, but at the same time were keen that their views remained anonymous. Some explicitly said that if they were identified, this could affect their chances of promotion and progression. The following quotes demonstrate this.

> I just want to be careful and be sure that I am not identified in the research, but I want you to be able to use my quotes in the research but would not want myself or my university to be identified. I don't think that would go down very well with my colleagues and I could be seen as someone who is causing issues to arise to the surface that many academics may not wish to discuss.

> I think these issues are very important and need to be identified and universities should be thinking about issues of inclusion and how racial inclusion works at all levels. I think I want to be careful that I am quoted and would like you to use my examples but to ensure that my role and what I do is not identified – because I could be identified and that would mean then that the university is also identified. There are troubling aspects of race that would not be seen in a sympathetic ways by my colleagues or my faculty.

Whilst the interviews were conducted to be as neutral as possible, there are always issues which may arise during the interview. 'An interview is contextual and negotiated. Whether participants recount their concerns without interruption or researchers request specific information, the result is a construction-or reconstruction-of a reality' (Charmaz, 2006: 27). Murphy and Dingwall (2003) suggest that interviews do not necessarily reproduce prior realities, 'rather these stories provide accounts from particular points of view that serve specific purposes, including assumptions that one should follow tactics and conversational rules during the interview' (Murphy and Dingwall, 2003: 27). There are always particular impressions that arise during the course of the interview. Sometimes these may be based on the individual identity of the researcher or the respondent and, when these issues arise, it is the researcher who must learn to adapt and assess the situation. When this happens respondents may seek cues from the researcher as to how to continue and which aspects to explore further, particularly if sensitive issues arise in the interview. This can also be related to power in the research relationship. I have argued elsewhere that power is based on a continuum, it shifts during the interview process and is based on a dynamic process and is present before, during and after the interview has been completed (Bhopal, 2010; see also Schwalbe and Wolkomir, 2002).

> Relative differences in power and status may be acted on and played out during an interview. Powerful people may take charge, turn the

interview questions to address topics on their own terms, and control the timing, pacing and length of the interview.
(Schwalbe and Wolkomir, 2002: 218)

Care has to be taken so that the researcher is aware of these issues and that the power does not shift completely to the researcher, or indeed to the respondent. There are also instances in which the respondent may hold the power by withholding information or respond in ways in which they think the researcher wants them to (see Bhopal, 2010). Powerful and non-powerful individuals alike may not feel comfortable or even 'trust' the interview situation and its process. Cohn and Lyons (2003: 46) argue that,

> Throughout the interpretive research process, power is not an item to be addressed in a research protocol, but an active force embedded in every methodological decision we make . . . since the research process is inherently unbalanced, researchers need to be attuned to issues of power throughout the research process.

Gender has also been identified as an issue which may affect the interview process. Whether the interviewer is a man interviewing a woman or a woman interviewing a woman, this may have an effect on the research relationship. 'When the interviewer is a man, gender dynamics may enter the interview. When the interviewer and participant are both women, class, age and/or race and ethnic differences may still influence how the interview proceeds' (Charmaz, 2006: 28). However, research suggests that women from different backgrounds are more likely than men to want to participate in interviews and are willing to discuss sensitive issues of their lives (Rheinharz and Chase, 2001).

Feminist research

Feminist research has been highly influential in how respondents participate and benefit from the research process. It has been instrumental in examining how we approach the research relationship: how we interpret the data and the extent to which we are reflexive about the research process. Feminists have criticised traditional research methods, particularly in relation to power and the need to address the emancipatory aspects of the research process in which research can be empowering for research participants, rather than for the benefit of the researchers conducting the research and collecting the data (Usher, 1996). Ezzy (2002: 43) suggests that gender is 'a category of experience' and that researchers must question the role of research and whether it empowers the oppressed or 'gives voice' to the marginalised. From this perspective, feminists have questioned the exploitative research relationship in which researchers are placed in positions of power (Jayaratne and Stewart, 1991); others have questioned who the research is for; individual gain rather than for the benefit of the respondents (Scott, 1985). Creswell (1998) has examined the extent to which feminist researchers should be conducting research on those who are less privileged and less powerful than themselves and whether this can be exploitative due to the unequal distribution of power in the research relationship (which is often favoured towards the researcher).

Feminist researchers suggest that the personal experiences of the researcher are a key part of the research. Ezzy (2002: 153) states that, 'the personal experience of the researcher is an integral part of the research process', claiming that objectivity is something that is rarely achieved in feminist research due to the personal, individual and subjective experiences of the researcher, and the effects these may have on the research process. Edwards and Mauthner (2002) argue that feminist research must examine how exploitative power relations are manifested within society so that the hierarchies between the respondents and the researcher can be questioned and explored, in order that equal power relations can be achieved. Consequently, feminists advocate a greater move towards participatory research methods which includes collaborative approaches (De Laine, 2000). De Laine suggests that participatory processes must exist at all levels of the research process from thinking about the research question, the methods, data collection, analysis, interpretation of data and how and where the research is disseminated. Other researchers have suggested that the research process is based on a Eurocentric perspective, one that is explored from a White, Western perspective (Thapar-Björkert and Henry, 2004). For example Thapar-Björkert and Henry (2004) demonstrate how participants can exercise a great deal of power in the research process and can use this to their advantage. Other feminists suggest using personal narratives as a method for exploring sensitive issues, but in this process respondents must not lose sight of the political aspects of their research and the effect it has on the wider community and society in general (Lather, 1991). Research that feminists are involved in must either have the potential to make some difference and lead to changes in society or, indeed, to have some impact on the communities that they are researching (Gillies and Alldred, 2002).

Whilst many feminists have privileged the use of qualitative research methods, others have suggested that quantitative methods can also have benefits for conducting feminist research (De Laine, 2000). De Laine (2000) suggests that feminists cannot assume that power differences and exploitation do not exist in the use of qualitative methods, and Gillies and Alldred (2002) suggest that feminist research can be problematic as it can involve a misuse of power (particularly when researching sensitive and personal issues) as well as in the interpretation and generation of specific meanings from the narratives provided by respondents.

Sensitivity in research is also an important issue that needs to be considered. Lee defines sensitive research as research, 'which potentially poses a substantial threat to those who are involved or have been involved in it' (Lee, 1993: 4). These could include intrusion into individual's private lives; a risk to individual careers; a threat to family members as well as aspects of cross-cultural factors in the research (Lee, 1993).

Black feminist research

A criticism of much of the writing on feminist research methods is their viewpoint from a White, Eurocentric perspective. Consequently, there have been many criticisms of the use of the term 'feminist research' by Black feminists (Brah, 1996; Phoenix, 2001; Gunaratnam, 2003; Bhopal, 2010). Feminist theorists contend that knowledge is socially situated and that Black women are positioned as marginalised outsiders (Hartsock, 1987; Harding, 1991). Collins (1990) uses the concept of 'outsider within' to explore how Black women occupy a position of privilege and power whilst simultaneously occupying a position that is marginalised by not being afforded the full rights of the privileges associated with being an insider, particularly when they are positioned in the academy. Brown (2012: 21) states, 'As agents of knowledge, Black women draw from their lived experiences, placed within a particular set of material, historical and epistemological conditions, to anchor specific knowledge claims'. Brown also reminds us that Black women in the academy face challenges as 'outsiders within', 'as marginalised academics whose standpoint uniquely equips them to uncover aspects of reality and truth that are concealed, unnoticed and masked by conventional methodological and epistemological frameworks and that they are reminded of their marginality in academic settings' (Brown, 2012: 21). It is the positionality of Black women that is unique which includes, 'historical, geographical, cultural, psychic and imaginative boundaries that provide ground for political definition and self-definition' (Lewis 2000: 173).

Reflexivity

Researchers' subjective experiences are part of the research process and consequently research is rarely objective:

> Qualitative researchers involve themselves in every aspect of their work. Through their eyes, data are developed and interpreted. Through their eyes, meaning is brought from an amalgam of words, images and interpretations. Through their eyes a creative work comes into fruition . . . our work is an expression of who we are and who we are becoming.
> (Lichtman, 2010: 121)

Others have argued that this individual subjectivity that we bring to the research process gives the research greater meaning as we begin to appreciate our own role as researchers within it (Haskell et al., 2002; Mehra, 2002).

Some writers suggest that researchers should think about moving away from traditional approaches towards research by adopting 'a decentred and reflexive position' so that the researcher can stand back and think about how their individuality affects the research process (Breuer and Roth, 2003: 17).

Reflexivity is a process that always exists in the research process (Rossman and Rallis, 2003). It involves a process of self-examination from the point of view of the researcher and it is based on the thoughts and actions of the researcher before, during and after the research has taken place (Russell and Kelly, 2002). It enables the researcher to think about their own positionality, their thoughts, feelings and attitudes towards their respondents and the research process. As Macbeth states, 'reflexivity has become a signal topic in contemporary discussions of qualitative research, especially in educational studies' (Macbeth, 2001: 35). Pillow (2003) argues that reflexivity should enable researchers to think about the self in the research process, but also the 'other' so that we can recognise uncomfortable practices which may enable us to explore the complexities and dilemmas in the research process. Others have suggested that it is in the data analysis process that we must consider issues of reflexivity (Pyett, 2003).

Many feminists support the notion of non-oppressive and non-hierarchal relationships in the research process (Rheinharz, 1992; Josselson, 1996) in which self-disclosure becomes part of the process of identifying our relationship to respondents and the process of how we conduct our research (Arvay, 1998). Reinharz states that, 'researchers who self-disclose are formulating the researcher's role in a way that maximises engagement of the self but also increases the researcher's vulnerability to criticism, both for what is revealed and for the very act of self-disclosure' (Reinharz, 1992: 34). Others have suggested that researchers consider the moral and emotional aspects of their research (Behar, 1996).

> We need to include ourselves in our research texts in visible ways in order for the reader to discern our interpretations . . . reflecting on the process of self-disclosure and its impact on knowledge production during the research encounter is a starting place.
> (Lichtman, 2010: 123)

This chapter has outlined the research methodology. It has provided background information on the different types of universities in the UK and the USA and data on the characteristics of respondents who participated in the research. The chapter has outlined the particular methodological approach that was taken in relation to ethical considerations, identity and positionality in the research. The following chapter will provide a critical understanding of race and identity in the academy. It will specifically explore the positioning of BME academics and how this is affected by their gender, race, class and aspects of power. It will draw upon empirical research to examine how identities are translated within the context of higher education by focusing specifically on the experiences of those working in the USA.

Note

1 http://lrsv.umd.edu/abstracts/Saumure_Given.pdf.

References

Aday L. (1996) *Designing and Conducting Health Surveys*. San Francisco, CA: Jossey-Bass.

Arvay, M. (1998) Struggling with re-presentation, voice and self in narrative research. Available from: http://www.edu.uvic.ca/connections/Conn98/arvay.html [Accessed 15 May 2014].

Bailey, K. (1988) Ethical dilemmas in social problems research. *American Sociologist*. 19 (2), pp.121–137.

Behar, R. (1996) *The Vulnerable Observer: Anthropology that breaks your heart*. Boston, MA: Beacon Press.

Benini, A. (2000) *The Construction of Knowledge*. Rome: Gnome Publishers.

Berg, B. (2007) *Qualitative Research Methods for the Social Sciences*. Boston, MA: Pearsons Education.

Bertrand, C. and Bourdeau, L. (2010) Research interviews by Skype: A new data collection method. In Esteves, J. (ed) *Proceedings from the 9th European Conference on Research Methods*. Spain: IE Business School, pp.70–79.

Bhopal, K. (2010) Gender, identity and experience: Researching marginalised groups. *Women's Studies International Forum*. 33 (1), pp.188–195.

Booth, C. (2008) Developing Skype-based reference services. *Internet Reference Services Quarterly*. 13, pp.147–165.

Brah, A. (1996) *Cartographies of Diaspora: Contesting identities*. London: Sage.

Breuer, F. and Roth, W. (2003) Subjectivity and reflexivity in the social sciences: Epistemic windows and methodical consequences. *Forum: Qualitative Social Research*. 12 (2), pp.12–25.

Brown, N. (2012) Negotiating the insider/outsider status: Black feminist ethnography and legislative studies. *Journal of Feminist Scholarship*. 3, pp.19–34.

Chapple A. (1999) The use of telephone interviewing for qualitative research. *Nurse Researcher*. 6, pp.85–93.

Charmaz, K. (2006) *Constructing Grounded Theory*. Thousand Oaks, CA: Sage.

Cohn, E. and Lyons, K. (2003) The perils of power in interpretive research. *American Journal of Occupational Therapy*. 57, pp.40–48.

Collins, P. (1990) *Black Feminist Thought: Knowledge, consciousness, and the politics of empowerment*. Boston, MA: UnwinHyman.

Creswell, J. (1998) *Qualitative Inquiry and Research Design: Choosing among five traditions*. Thousand Oaks, CA: Sage.

Davidson, A. (2002) *Grounded Theory – Defined* [Online] Available from: http://www.essortment.com/all/groundedtheory_rmnf.htm [Accessed 18 May 2014].

De Laine, M. (2000) *Fieldwork, Participation and Practice*. Oxford: Oxford University Press.

Dujardin, A. (2009) Conversations with an e-learner. *Brookes eJournal of Learning and Teaching*. Available from: http://bejlt.brookes.ac.uk/article/conversations_with_an_e_learner/ [Accessed 12 July 2014].

Edwards, R. and Mauthner, M. (2002) Ethics and feminist research: Theory and practice. In Mauthner, M., Birch, M., Jessop, J. and Miller, T. (eds) *Ethics in Qualitative Research*. London: Sage, pp.14–31.

Ezzy, D. (2002) *Qualitative Analysis: Practice and innovation*. Crows Nest, NSW: Allen & Unwin.

Fontana, A. and Frey, J. (1994) Interviewing: The art of science. In Denzin, N. and Lincoln, Y. (eds) *Handbook of Qualitative Research*. Thousand Oaks, CA: Sage, pp.361–376.

Fontana, A. and Frey, J. (2008) The interview: From neutral stance to political involvement. In Denzin, N. and Lincoln, Y. (eds) *Collecting and Interpreting Qualitative Materials*. Los Angeles, CA: Sage, pp.137–149.

Frey, J. (1989) *Survey Research by Telephone*. Newbury Park, CA: Sage.

Gillies, V. and Alldred, P. (2002) The ethics of intention: Research as a political tool. In Mauthner, M., Birch, M., Jessop, J. and Miller, T. (eds) *Ethics in Qualitative Research*. London: Sage, pp.35–52.

Glaser, B. and Strauss, A. (1967) *The Discovery of Grounded Theory*. Chicago: Aldine Publishing Company.

Gunaratnam, Y. (2003) *Researching Race and Ethnicity*. London: Sage.

Harding, S. (1991) *Whose Science? Whose knowledge? Thinking from women's lives*. Milton Keynes: Open University Press.

Hartsock, N. (1987) The feminist standpoint: Developing the ground for a specifically feminist historical materialism. In Harding, S. (ed) *Feminism and Methodology*. Bloomington: Indiana University Press, pp. 157–180.

Haskell, J., Linds, W. and Ippolito, J. (2002) Opening spaces of possibility: The enactive as a qualitative research approach. *Forum: Qualitative Social Research*. Available from: http://www.qualitative-research.net [Accessed 23 May 2014].

Hine, C. (2004) Social research methods and the internet: A thematic review. *Sociological Research Online*. Available from: http://www.socresonline.org.uk /9/2/hine.html> doi:10.5153/sro.924 [Accessed 18 May 2014].

Jayaratne, T. and Stewart, A. (1991) Quantitative and qualitative methods in the social sciences: Feminist issues and practical strategies. In Holland, J., Blair, M. and Sheldon, S. (eds) *Debates and Issues in Feminist Research and Pedagogy*. Clevedon, Somerset: Multilingual Matters, pp.217–234.

Josselson, R. (1996) *Ethics and Process in the Narrative Study of Lives*. London: Sage.

Kazmer, M. and Xie, B. (2008) Qualitative interviewing in internet studies: Playing with the media, playing with the method. *Information, Communication, and Society*. 11, pp.257–278.

Lather, P. (1991) *Getting Smart: Feminist research and pedagogy within the post-modern* New York: Routledge.

Lee, R. (1993) *Doing Research on Sensitive Topics*. London: Sage.

Lewis, G. (2000) *'Race', Gender and Social Welfare: Encounters in a postcolonial Society*. Cambridge: Polity.

Lichtman, M. (2010) *Qualitative Research Methods in Education*. Thousand Oaks, CA: Sage.

Lofland, J. and Lofland, L. (1995) *Analysing Social Settings: A guide to qualitative observation and analysis*. Belmont, CA: Wadsworth Publishing Company.

Macbeth, D. (2001) On 'reflexivity' in qualitative research. *Qualitative Inquiry*. 7 (1), pp.35–68.

Markham, A. (2008) The methods, politics, and ethics of representation in online ethnography. In Denzin, N. and Lincoln, Y. (eds) *Collecting and Interpreting Qualitative Materials*. Los Angeles, CA: Sage, pp.95–124.

Mehra, B. (2002) Bias in qualitative research: Voices from an online classroom. *The Qualitative Report*. Available from http://www.nova.edu/ssss/QR/QR7-1/mehra.html [Accessed 20 May 2014].

Murphy, E. and Dingwall, R. (2003) *Qualitative Methods and Health Policy Research.* New York: Aldine de Gruyter.

Phoenix, A. (2001) Including and excluding families, shifting constructions of 'race', class, gender and age. *Journal for Humanistics.* 7, pp.57–67.

Pillow, W. (2003) Confession, catharsis, or cure? Rethinking the uses of reflexivity as methodological power in qualitative research. *Qualitative Studies in Education.* 16 (2), pp.175–196.

Pfeiffer, D. (2000) The devils are in the details: The ICIDH2 and the disability movement. *Disability and Society.* 15 (7), pp.1078–1082.

Pyett, P. (2003) Validation of qualitative research in the real world. *Qualitative Health Research.* 13 (8), pp.1170–1179.

Rheinharz, S. (1992) *Feminist Methods in Social Research.* Oxford: Oxford University Press.

Reinharz, S. and Chase, S. (2001) Interviewing women. In Gubrium, J. and Holstein, J. (eds) *Handbook of Interview Research.* Thousand Oaks, CA: Sage Publications, pp.220–239.

Rossman, G. and Rallis, S. (2003) *Learning in the Field: An introduction to qualitative research.* Thousand Oaks, CA: Sage.

Russell, G. and Kelly, N. (2002) Research as interacting dialogic processes: Implications for reflexivity. *Forum: Qualitative Social Research.* Available from:http://www.qualitative-research.net/fqs-texte/3-02/3-02russellkelly-e.htm [Accessed 20 June 2014].

Schaefer, D. and Dillman, D. (1998) Development of a standard e-mail methodology. *Public Opinion Quarterly.* 62 (3), pp.378–379.

Samure, K. and Given, L. No date available: http://lrsv.umd.edu/abstracts/Saumure_Given.pdf. [Accessed 20 April 2014]

Sarantakos, S. (2005) *Social Research.* London: Palgrave Macmillan.

Schwalbe, M. and Wolkomir, M. (2002) Interviewing men. In Gubrium, J. and and Holstein, J. (eds) *Handbook of Interview Research.* Thousand Oaks, CA: Sage, pp.203–219.

Scott, S. (1985) Feminist research and qualitative methods: A discussion of some of the issues. In Burgess, R. (ed) *Issues in Educational Research: Qualitative methods.* London: Falmer Press, pp.67–85.

Sproull, N. (1988) *Handbook of Research Methods: A guide for practitioners and students in the social sciences.* Lanham, MD: Scarecrow Press.

Strauss, A. and Corbin, J. (1990) *Basics of Qualitative Research: Grounded theory procedures and techniques.* Newbury Park, CA: Sage.

Sturges, J. and Hanrahan, K. (2004) Comparing telephone and face-to-face qualitative interviewing: A research note. *Qualitative Research.* 4, pp.107–118.

Sullivan, J. (2012) Skype: An appropriate method of data collection for qualitative interviews?' *The Hilltop Review.* 6 (1), pp.956–961.

Sweet, L. (2002) Telephone interviewing: Is it compatible with interpretive phenomenological research? *Contemporary Nursing.* 12, pp.58–63.

Thapar-Björkert, S. and Henry, M. (2004) Reassessing the research relationship: Location, position and power in fieldwork accounts. *International Journal of Social Research Methodology.* 7 (5) pp.363–381.

Usher R. (1996) A critique of the neglected epistemological assumptions of educational research. In Scott, D. and Usher, R. (eds) *Understanding Educational Research.* London: Routledge, pp.90–105.

4 Theoretical understandings of identity in the academy

This chapter will provide a critical understanding of race and identity within the context of higher education. It will explore how BME academics are positioned in the academy by exploring aspects of gender, race, class and power. The chapter will draw upon data with respondents who were working in universities in the USA to examine how identities are translated within the context of higher education.

Leadership

Diversity and inclusion

Much of the literature that has explored aspects of social justice and inclusion from the perspective of social leaders has examined how social justice can work in relation to the functioning of leadership roles in organisations (Jean-Marie, 2010; Theoharis, 2010). Some research has examined how leaders are able to facilitate social justice within the classroom, particularly when classroom practices are focused around discourses of racism and anti-racism. Ryan states that, '... racism ought to be a serious concern for educational leaders, particularly those who hold positions of responsibility in schools, like principals and head teachers. This is because the place where racism is often most evident is at the school level' (2000: 14–15). Diem and Carpenter (2013) argue that leadership roles in education must be built around providing a critical dialogue in which anti-racist conversations are present in order that learning can take place in an inclusive environment.

Other researchers have suggested that diversity is a concept that should be embedded in all aspects of the school curriculum, at all levels (Milner, 2010). It should be taught as part of the curriculum, particularly for those involved in teacher training programmes in order that teachers are aware that diversity is an aspect that is embedded in their teaching, rather than an 'add on'. Diem and Carpenter (2013) have developed five critical concepts which can be developed as part of the curriculum and used as pedagogical practice, particularly in relation to preparing leaders to work in diverse settings. These perspectives explore a colour-blind ideology,[1] misconceptions of difference, merit-based achievement, critical self-reflection and the interrogation of race-related silences in the classroom (Diem and Carpenter, 2013: 2). The authors argue that it is critical for those in leadership roles to explore how inclusive practices and discourses of race and racism can affect teaching and learning processes in the classroom (Carpenter and Diem, 2012). An understanding of diversity becomes increasingly relevant given an increase in the diversity of the student body with universities attracting students from different national and international backgrounds. Consequently, those in leadership roles have a duty to explore how they manage and teach a diverse body of staff and students in traditionally White environments (Aud et al., 2012). Some researchers however have suggested that those in leadership roles do not value issues of race and racism as being relevant to their organisations (Ryan, 2003). 'The cultural, racial and ethnic divide between teachers, leaders and school communities make the examination of how leadership preparation programs equip leaders of diverse communities of paramount importance and presents a myriad of implications for academic achievement' (Diem and Carpenter, 2013: 4). There must be an emphasis on exploring colour-blind ideologies (particularly in relation to classroom and leadership practices) in order that racial differences amongst individuals are emphasised. Brown et al. state that some leaders may, '. . . oppose race-conscious solutions on the grounds that racial inclusion requires only that individuals be treated similarly under the law – no more, no less' (2003: 4), whereas Bonilla-Silva describes this process as 'colour-blind racism' which is 'racism lite' (2010). However, Diem and Carpenter argue that this idea of colour blind ideology is disadvantageous for those from minority backgrounds. 'Research has shown that using a colour-blind discourse not only allows Whiteness to remain invisible as the measure of comparison to other races/ethnicities, it also disavows the importance of the histories and cultures of underrepresented groups' (2013: 6). Schofield (2010) has also argued that a colour-blind ideology may actually misrepresent the realities of racism and consequently promote feelings of racism and prejudice towards individuals of colour.

> Educational leaders and programs preparing them must be familiar with the theoretical constructs of colour blind ideologies . . . Today the reproduction of White privilege and racial structures continue to exist so those in power are able to maintain their privilege and benefit from a position of dominance.
> (Diem and Carpenter, 2013: 7)

Milner (2010) asserts that it is important to recognise that students enter education from different economic, educational and social backgrounds and that, for some, discriminatory practices continue to shape the opportunities they have available to them. Diem and Carpenter state,

While the field of educational leadership has often addressed the importance of *why* a socially conscious and critical reflective pedagogy is important, there must be a more concerted effort to examine *how* this type of pedagogy can be developed and implemented within leadership preparation programs.

(2013: 11, original emphasis)

The authors also recognise the importance of race and racism and how these issues affect leadership programmes in teaching. '*The critical examination of issues pertaining to race and racism must be a central component to all courses within leadership preparation programs*' (2013: 13, original emphasis). They also state that it is within the field of leadership that changes must be made and instigated so that those in leadership positions can make significant changes at all levels. '*Scholars within the field of educational leadership must conduct research efforts that move beyond the naming of race-related problems by conducting research efforts that contribute to the active development and implementation of anti-racist strategies in the classroom*' (2013: 15, original emphasis).

Gender

There has been a great deal of research which has explored the effects of gender on leadership roles. Research suggests that Black women in senior leadership roles in the USA are underrepresented, particularly in predominantly White institutions (Jackson and O'Callaghan, 2009) and there are greater numbers of women of colour than men of colour in higher educational administration roles. Some researchers have argued that women of colour continue to experience disadvantages related to their 'token' status and their positions are not regarded or judged as equal to those of their White colleagues in the academy. Consequently, these stereotypical positions of women of colour continue to have a negative influence on their position as leaders in the academy (Sanchez-Hucles and Davis, 2010). Lloyd-Jones states, '. . . the absence or presence of racially or ethnically diverse administrators in academe communicates a message to students, faculty and other administrators of colour, which can affect their feelings of welcome and a sense of belonging' (2011: 4).

There have been particular areas which have been identified as having negative impacts for Black people in senior leadership administrative roles. These include access, retention and career advancement, particularly for those who are in senior positions at predominantly White institutions (Bennefield, 1990). Lloyd-Jones states,

Changing demographics, retention of students and advancement of faculty and administrators of colour provide sound rationale for principally White institutions to implement strategies and engage in practices

> that eliminate institutional, social and internal impediments, thereby diversifying the executive-level administrative ranks of higher education in terms of gender, race and ethnicity.
>
> (2011: 4)

Lloyd-Jones (2011) also argues that those from Black backgrounds, particularly women, continue to experience a diverse range of disadvantages compared to their White colleagues.

> The terms double jeopardy, dual burden, double bind and interactive discrimination have been used interchangeably to connote a set of conflicting expectations and pressures that may be created when an individual is considered to have membership in two distinct minority groups.
>
> (2011: 5)

Significant changes in the population demographics of the USA demonstrate that the numbers of Black students enrolling for college have significantly increased, at the same time as the numbers of ethnic minority individuals in the population are steadily increasing. By 2050, the number of people of colour is predicted to be 50% of the US population (US Census Bureau, 2010). 'Currently over 27 million women of colour are in the workforce and the US Census Bureau has predicted that Whites, long considered the majority, will drop below 50% of the population by the year 2050' (Lloyd-Jones, 2011: 8). Whilst there has been an increase in the numbers of women of colour in leadership roles, they remain under represented in senior roles in general, particularly in senior decision making roles. (Sanchez-Hucles and Sanchez, 2007). Research suggests that women of colour in leadership roles have to contend with continuous stereotypes about their work and their status which often leads to racial and sexual stereotyping (Madden, 2005). This is related to their 'token status' and the knowledge that their White colleagues expect them to attain unrealistic goals. These stereotypes contribute to reinforcing negative outcomes for women of colour, particularly in relation to their multiple identities (Collins, 1990). Hoyt (2007) suggests that Black African American women may experience particular stereotypes because of their class, gender and racial identities, leading to greater negative experiences compared to their White colleagues. Many Black women have little access to professional networks and possibilities for advancement compared to their White colleagues, which may hinder their progress for advancement in higher education.

An understanding of leadership in the academy focuses on the use of different leadership styles (such as effective and ineffective leadership styles), different leadership practices and skills and aspects of appearance and behaviour.

Research from a socially constructivist perspective has provided evidence that leadership is socially constructed and that the frameworks and assumptions of individuals affect what they perceive to be effective leadership, the way leaders enact their role, and the relationship between leaders and followers.

(Lloyd-Jones, 2011: 15)

Eagly and Chin (2010) emphasise that analysing leadership should also include the experiences of those who remain marginalised and do not have access to positions of power and privilege in society.

Race and educational inequalities

Research suggests an increase in the numbers of women of colour who are earning doctoral degrees (NCES, 2009), but at the same time, women of colour remain underrepresented in the academy and experience obstacles to success (Turner, 2008). Mertz (2011: 42) states, ' . . . less attention has been directed to the entry and induction processes of higher education for females of colour, and the ways in which the culture of the academy make these processes vulnerable to covert, if not overt bias and discrimination'. There have been particular theories which have examined how the subordinate position of those from marginalised groups operates in the academy. For example, Critical Theory as developed by Habermas (1998) and Marcuse (1968) explores how the inequalities of power work in different institutions which continue to reproduce inequalities. This results in some groups having a dominant role compared to others as well as through a process of privileging some groups over others in which the norms and values of the dominant group are accepted as the correct mode of conduct (Apple, 2006). Mertz states,

> long standing norms and values rooted in white, male western ideology are privileged in the academy and sanctioned by long use. They dominate the culture and ways of thinking and are perpetuated through their institutionalisation in the structure and the way in which individuals are selected and socialised within the academy.
>
> (2011: 46)

Mertz suggests that the norms and values of the dominant group are so embedded within the culture of the academy that they form part of the worldview of those who are part of the academy, which also contributes to hidden biases in recruitment processes in the academy, ' . . . and the subtlety of these biases allows institutions and many within them to believe they are virtually 'colour-blind' above distinctions of race, ethnicity, gender and sexual orientation' (2011: 46). This often takes place through hidden processes which provide, 'the opportunity to enact one's privilege to perpetuate others' oppression' (Ropers-Huilman, 2008: 47).

Recruitment processes

There has been a great deal of research which has explored the role of search committees and their role in recruitment processes. Much of the research suggests that search committees operate to perpetuate current norms of behaviour and reproduce the status quo. 'The committee will reify the status quo in representation and thinking, easily agreeing to interpretations of qualifications that replicate the existing membership, and disadvantage the applicants that are different from them' (Mertz, 2011: 47). Turner and Myers (2000) suggest that those from Black and marginalised backgrounds may be disadvantaged in the selection processes conducted by search committees, as their areas of research (such as diversity and inequality) may not be seen as appealing to them. Mertz argues that in this process of selection, a 'network of knowns' operates to include those from White backgrounds who are seen to 'fit in' with the traditional norms of the faculty. 'The tradition of getting new hires through the network of knowns continues today and remains one of the most influential ways in which candidates are recommended for positions' (2011: 50). Furthermore, many faculties emphasise the 'fit' of the candidate with the department or faculty. 'It has been suggested that fit with the organisation is a more important factor in determining who gets the job than the requirements of the job and is integral to the discourse on hiring practices and personnel decisions' (Tooms et al., 2009: 96). Tooms et al. (2009) suggest that search committees make decisions early on in the search process (quite often even before they have met the candidate) such as whether a candidate will fit in with their faculty, their outlook and attitudes and replicate their values, norms and behaviour. For example,

> For female faculty of colour, their gender, race and ethnicity are obvious factors in establishing their difference from the norm, real and imagined, and leads to their being subjected to a more intense scrutiny in determining their fit than a candidate who more closely resembles the norm.
>
> (Mertz, 2011: 54)

Others have suggested that some universities can be seen as unwelcoming and alienating for people of colour (Gallagher and Trower, 2009). As Mertz suggests,

> To be successful in academic terms, attain tenure and promotion, principally requires being socialised into the roles and expectations for the position – both of which owe much to traditional academic norms – by

those who have successfully been socialised and have earned the right to make judgements about the legitimacy and appropriateness of those who have newly entered the academy.

(2011: 59)

Uzzi (1997) argues that this may be related to people of colour not having access to informal support networks which can provide greater access to promotion and tenure, which are often the most influential factors in this process. Mertz suggests that universities must improve their search practices if they are to be truly inclusive for those who remain marginalised.

It is all too easy for institutions to delude themselves into thinking that rhetoric and policies which speak to non-discrimination, and checklists designed to remind people that they should be inclusive will achieve the desired changes in climate and behaviour to which they say they are committed. Institutions must be committed to change, truly committed, and willing to confront their failure to achieve the desired diversity and supportive climate for diversity.

(2011: 63)

Mentoring programmes

Research that has explored the importance of mentoring networks in the success of men and women of colour in senior positions in the academy suggests that women experience greater disadvantages compared to men and so require greater access to mentoring programmes than men (Young and Brooks, 2008). Women of colour are viewed as 'outsiders' in the White academy and consequently are less likely to have access to such networks (Gibson, 2006). Jean-Marie and Brooks suggest that, 'Mentoring networks are vital support structures in a successful academic career, as emerging scholars seek to navigate the complex and protean racial and gender dynamics of academic institutions' (2011: 92). It has been suggested that mentoring can provide formal and informal support networks which can increase productivity at the same time as providing emotional and social support (Gibson, 2006). Mentoring usually involves an experienced individual who is able to provide guidance and support for those who have are less experienced. Diggs et al. (2009: 331) argue that mentoring can provide aspects of informal support for people of colour in 'the coloured space' in which individuals feel safe in receiving support. Seibert et al. suggest that social networks play an important role in networking relationships. 'A social network is the pattern of ties linking a defined set of persons or social actors and each person can be described in terms of his or her links with other people in the network' (2001: 219). Jean-Marie and Brooks emphasise that,

> Women of faculty of colour are likely to develop a network of colleagues and support systems with similar characteristics (such as age, race, gender and discipline) in which they disseminate information to each other and where other members may have already received the information.
>
> (2011: 98)

Mentoring networks have been shown to be very important for women of colour if they want to progress in their careers,

> Mentoring relationships can go a long way toward helping faculty women of colour overcome entrenched barriers to their success. Whilst it is important for faculty women of colour to have proactive and supportive mentors, it is equally important for them to take the initiative and create their own networks that serve multiple formal and informal processes.
>
> (Jean-Marie and Brooks, 2011: 105)

Mitchell and Miller (2011) discuss the 'unwritten rules' which women of colour have to learn and adhere to in order to be successful in the academy. They have to do so by developing a 'professional persona' by which they will be judged.

> Genuine mentoring programs with mentors who thoroughly understand the plight of marginalised women scholars and actively champion women of colour would make great strides toward equaling the inequitable path women of color in academia currently tred on the road to senior, tenured academic positions.
>
> (Mitchell and Miller, 2011: 214)

As the academy has traditionally been the preserve of White middle class men, Black women have to overcome particular barriers related to 'gendered performances' in the academy (Lester, 2008). The importance of networking is seen as crucial in this process, particularly in relation to how Black women present themselves and how they use their networks as sources of support for career promotion and progression. Bass and Faircloth (2011) discuss this in relation to 'academic power':

> . . . the power of influence to control and dominate occurrences and outcomes in academe. Academic power is manifested in having control over publication outlets, holding leadership roles in prominent institutions and organisations, having a well-established reputation and name recognition, having attained the distinction of full professor at a research intensive university, having a lengthy publication record and being well connected to others who possess similar levels of academic success.
>
> (2011: 223)

Jones (2011: 272) relates academic power to types of knowledge that are accepted in the academy.

> Individuals from the dominant group in power in universities determine what counts as valuable knowledge and appropriate research methods and define what is included in the circle of valuable knowledge. The distinction typically excludes research areas of interest to faculty of colour that focus on issues of equity, race, ethnicity and racism.

The remaining sections will explore empirical data on the positioning of BME academics in the academy; whether Black African American academics felt accepted in the academy; the importance of support networks and mentoring programmes in the success of academics, and how intersectionalities of difference had an effect on the experiences of Black African American academics working in universities in the USA.

The empirical data: US respondents

There were clear differences between respondents from the USA and those from the UK when they spoke about aspects of identity in relation to how they were positioned in the academy. Many of the respondents from the USA compared the identity of Whiteness to their identity of 'being Black' and 'Blackness' as a political identity. Many were overtly political in their responses and referred to political activism in their academic lives – an identity which they related as being part of their intellectual self. Issues of race and inclusion were more likely to be seen as political processes rather than as intellectual or academic processes, though both were clearly linked. Many of the respondents identified the USA as being more progressive than the UK in terms of an understanding of race, identity and racial politics. Respondents from the USA reported a sense of greater equity at their institutions compared to those from the UK, particularly in relation to their universities working towards creating a sense of inclusion and social justice. This was identified by a greater participation in political action, for example some of the respondents referred to Black Power movements and leaders such as Malcolm X as being particularly positive in shaping their identities in higher education. Others referred to the fact that many universities offered graduate and postgraduate courses on African American Studies and Black History courses, something which was not offered in the UK. Many UK respondents felt a greater sense of marginalisation which was reflected in the failure to appreciate that Black history was not intellectually recognised through the teaching of courses which provided a historical grounding of race, diversity and inclusion.

Researching race

Many of the respondents in the USA (like their UK counterparts) were researching issues of race, diversity and inclusion. Several commented that this area of work was one that they were passionate about and one which they wanted to use to make a difference in how race and racism was understood. Others spoke about some of the 'difficulties' associated with researching race, diversity and inclusion and how it was judged by their White colleagues. Many respondents suggested that researching race and diversity was once the sole preserve of BME academics, but recently this had begun to change with greater numbers of White academics studying the area. Many respondents spoke about the importance of being able to share their work with other Black academics who could understand and empathise with it.

> I mostly like being surrounded by a critical mass of colleagues who share my commitment to diversity and social justice and are invested in working to bring about needed change both in and outside of the institution. There seem to be more and more non-BME colleagues who are interested in these areas and that is ok, as long as we are working for the same cause (Black, female full professor).

As many of the USA respondents were working on areas of race, social justice and equality issues some felt they were misjudged because of this, by their White colleagues.

> They [White colleagues] are pleasant on the surface, but I feel very few consider me a colleague. Because my work is more geared towards activist and grounded theory research, many in my department don't consider it valid (Black, male full professor).

Others felt that their topics of research were 'tolerated' and 'accepted' rather than respected.

> People are pleasant to my face, but rarely do they engage with me about my work. They always want to talk to me when they become flustered around issues to do with race and that worries me. If there is something going on in the faculty that has to do with race, they will seek me out to make sure that I can help them. Because I am a Black African American they think my face fits (Black, male assistant professor).

A Black female assistant professor gave an interesting perspective on how she was 'positioned' in her university and her faculty.

> I think people situate me at the university in a couple of different ways. On the one hand, I am positioned as the 'face' of the university

to students, faculty and communities of colour. Also, my perspective, experiences and points of view are valued because they provide some insight into the experiences of faculty of colour throughout the university. Occasionally I am asked to speak to visiting students and faculty of colour, to serve on diversity-focussed committees and to counsel students of colour. On the other hand, I'm at times asked or expected to participate in discussions about diversity – and even equity – though many of my colleagues share similar interests and commitments. While this type of participation is not rewarded in ways that publications and research are rewarded, my commitment to these issues means that I do at times provide this service.

The expectation that some respondents had to perform this role was immense, yet it did not have the same respect or importance attached to it as research and scholarship. However, respondents were expected by their colleagues to provide this service *because* they were Black.

Acceptance in the academy?

Many of the respondents in the USA discussed their feelings of acceptance and non-acceptance in the White space of the academy. On the one hand they realised that they faced different challenges to their White colleagues, such as their positioning within their faculties as Black academics and how their work was valued and judged in comparison to that of their White colleagues. Yet on the other hand, there were several strategies they used in order to be accepted in the academy, one of which included the recognition that they would always occupy a dual position as 'outsiders' at the same time as being 'insiders'. This included the importance of maintaining a professional persona such as meeting deadlines, being on time and attending meetings, teaching to the highest standards and aiming to publish in high quality journals. Many respondents felt the bar of achievement was raised higher for Black academics compared to the expectations placed on White colleagues. Consequently, respondents felt they had to perform to the highest levels in order to avoid criticism from their White colleagues.

> I do try and want to be accepted by my White colleagues, but I think that that is a very difficult process to go through. There is acceptance at all kinds of levels because you want to be accepted as being part of the faculty and because of your work. But that is not always the case because acceptance can come in various ways. It also depends on which university and faculty department you are in. Some are more accepting than others. This is often based on who is the chairperson in that faculty and how that process of acceptance works for you. That acceptance is also based on your performance because you know that you have to do

> better than them [White colleagues] because if you don't you stand out and they have something against you. We are probably our own worst enemies because we always feel we have to do better than everyone else, but we are left no choice but to do this – otherwise we will be seen as failures (Black, female assistant professor).

Other respondents related their acceptance to the type of research they conducted and how this was influential in whether their colleagues accepted them.

> It often depends on what your area of interest and expertise is. Some of your colleagues do accept you and others don't. If there is a critical mass of other colleagues working in a similar area to you, you may be accepted but you may still be the outsider because of your race. You will always stand out. On the other hand you could be seen as not being accepted because your area is different to that of others and so colleagues may not understand what it is that you are interested in. Levels of acceptance happen in different ways and different forms (Black, female professor).

A Black, female associate professor spoke about how she used her appearance and presentation of self to increase her acceptance by her colleagues in her faculty.

> As a female of colour I have to ensure that I am representing other females of colour in my communities so I ensure that I dress to be accepted. If I were to turn up in sweats that would not help. I dress in a professional and smart manner to ensure that my peers and colleagues see me as someone who is serious about her work and who takes her work seriously. I also want my students to respect me and also to see me as a positive role model. Being a woman of colour and one who has not had a privileged upbringing means that I have to have some acceptance in how I am seen, so I go to great lengths and great efforts to look professional at all times. This means I can present this persona to my colleagues and my students and it gives me more confidence.

Many of the respondents spoke about maintaining their professional persona and how it affected how they would be judged by their colleagues and students; particularly in relation to their dress and physical appearance. Many also spoke about the need to feel respected by their colleagues so that they were seen as 'credible'. This notion of 'credibility' was often associated with how senior managers would judge colleagues. Some respondents mentioned the notion of 'credibility' in relation to applying for, and being awarded promotions.

Understandings of identity in the academy

> I was told that before I apply for my tenured full professor post, I had to make sure I had the credibility. I am not convinced that I know what that means; does it mean that they can judge me to be worthy that is that I can become a full professor because they accept me as being one? I am not sure what this means? I asked my Dean, does it not have to do with meeting a set of criteria and showing eligibility for that? If that is the case, then how does this vague concept of credibility fit into that? I am still not convinced what it means. Credibility comes from how others see you and how others judge you and that is a subjective experience, so how can it be measured, what are the criteria? How can it be used in promotion processes? It is too vague and is based on subjectivity, one person may see you as being credible to take the title of full professor, but another person may not (Black, female associate professor).

Others spoke about the notion of 'acceptance' before they could apply for their full professorship, which was also related to the concept of 'credibility'.

> There is an unspoken rule here that in this faculty one has to be accepted by the faculty, its members and those in power before one can be seen to be part of that club. The club is the elite and it's the one that makes most of the decisions and is involved in the decisions making process. How does that acceptance work? It is often if they know you or if your face fits and they want to know you. It's also about if they want you to be part of that club. If you look at it from that perspective, then being a person of colour you are automatically disadvantaged. There is in some sense a need for White academics to keep their own positions of power and not to let people of colour impose or infringe on that White space, because it is for them – and them only (Black, male professor).

These feelings of 'credibility' and 'acceptance' were also related to Black academics positioned as 'outsiders' in the academy. The notion of 'fitting in' was related to different aspects of 'being part of the club' and being accepted by White colleagues.

> We are very conscious of background here in the US and this is often seen as a signifier of who you are, a marker of difference because it does matter where you come from and what your roots are. Some of my colleagues in this organisation have studied at prestigious colleges such as the Ivy League and they come from very affluent backgrounds where there are different ways of doing things and that makes a difference to ordinary people like us – people of colour – who have always been disadvantaged to some extent. So one's background can and does influence the level of acceptance in the faculty and as a woman of colour I feel that our acceptance is challenging and defined in terms that are different to the majority of my colleagues here (Latina, female assistant professor).

Others spoke about being accepted by their students and how this was an important factor in how they were in turn, judged by their colleagues.

> Acceptance is also about having respect from the students. They are the ones who look up to you and many of the students of colour here look up to us – to the professors of colour – because they see them in positions of power and in positions where they can contribute to change and influence how decisions are made and many students of colour appreciate that. This is something that they need. We have a great representation of people of colour at professorial levels here, but we need more. It's only then can we make a real difference to be inclusive if our students can benefit from that inclusion. If you are accepted by the students and they respect you, then that can be translated to staff who also have to note that student acceptance and respect counts for a lot (Black, male professor).

Other strategies respondents used to 'get on' in the academy included the use of support and mentoring networks.

Support networks

Respondents spoke about how despite their experiences of feeling marginalised and excluded in the White space of the academy, one of the ways in which they overcame these negative aspects was to develop specific networks of support which they used to enable them to succeed. These networks of support from their colleagues and peers provided them with emotional, academic and instrumental support. Many said that these support networks operated outside of their university. One Black, female assistant professor spoke about how her support networks had an important positive effect on her success in higher education.

> I work in an environment that is predominantly White. This may be because of the type of university it is; it has a high status and is seen as very research intensive and prestigious. So it is predominantly White. There are not many people of colour here and as a female woman of colour, I will automatically go to other people of colour for support and conversation but because there are few here, it is harder to do. My support networks come from outside of my university and those support networks are also men and women of colour who have experienced some of the issues I have experienced. This gives us a sense of belonging and we support each other when we need to, we are there for each other. Most importantly we pick each other up when we are told we are not very good or our research is not worthy. That is what makes a difference, if I didn't have that it would be very difficult for me. The support I receive from other Black people of colour has contributed to my success; it has given me confidence when I have needed that confidence the most.

The support took different forms; it was either face to face, telephone, Skype or email contact. The continuity of support was vital for its success.

> I had an issue with a member of staff here who was behaving in such a way that it was a form of bullying and I couldn't speak to my colleagues in the faculty because this was a senior member of staff and it would have been sensitive. So I spoke to my Black colleague who is working a thousand miles away from me. We had a conversation that meant I could discuss with her the different aspects of the situation and there was no need to worry about what I was going to say. I mentioned that I thought it could be racism and exclusion and I thought this was happening because I am a female of colour. I could do that without being judged, but knowing that I could pick up the phone or Skype her again if I wanted to was very important for me, it is that regular contact that makes the difference and makes you feel as though you are really being supported (Black, female assistant professor).

Support was also based on academic input, such as the value of having colleagues who would read draft articles for publication, advise which journals to publish in and which mechanisms were successful for applying for funding – all of which were crucial in gaining promotion and tenure. However, the most important aspect of support that was mentioned was access to colleagues and networks which would offer individuals opportunities for career progression such as significant opportunities for increased visibility in the academy which could contribute to promotion and tenure.

> The most important type of support I have received is having access to a couple of experienced professors who have read my portfolio for my full professorship. They have also been through the process and know what to look for and can also examine and see some of the aspects that I need to highlight. Receiving these comments has been very beneficial to me, but this is something I am not sure I could ask colleagues in my faculty to do. They are also people 'in the know', they are experienced and have connected me to people I would never have met and have given me the opportunity to deliver keynotes, edit books and sit on editorial boards and these are things I would never have had the opportunity to do. For many people of colour these networks simply do not exist and so our opportunities can be limited (Black, female associate professor).

One respondent who researched social justice and racial inclusion was one of a few members of staff in his faculty who worked in this area of research. Consequently, he relied on the support he received from his Black colleagues in different institutions. This support included feedback on his publications and critical insight and advice on which journals to publish in.

> Because of the type of areas that I work in many colleagues in my faculty would not know which journals I should publish in. So I ask my Black colleagues who are in other universities. They are able to advise me and they are also able to comment on my work. If I did not have that kind of support I am not sure how I would get on. There are some White colleagues here who would offer me support, but I am not convinced they know enough about my area (Black, male assistant professor).

Others spoke about how the advice they received had a direct impact on their career decisions.

> When you first start out you are not so sure about certain things and you need to know who it is that you can ask about those things which you are unsure or unclear about. There are many people who have been helpful here in my university, but I tend to want to speak to those who are from a similar background to me and who can understand some of the issues that I am experiencing as a female woman of colour – having that understanding is very important to me. It means there are certain things that I don't have to explain and these are often those things that are taken for granted (Black, female assistant professor).

A significant number of respondents mentioned a greater affinity with those who were from similar backgrounds to themselves, particularly when understanding aspects of race and racism and how this worked in the academy. Many expressed the notion that their White colleagues were unable to empathise with them and so could not quite understand the processes of exclusion that operated on subtle, conscious and unconscious levels. Others discussed support as having access to a 'network of knowns': a means of providing access to different types of networks, such as educational organisations which provided them with information and access to opportunities. One respondent spoke about how her connection with a senior Black African American male professor had led her to increase her profile and enhance her presence in the academy. This notion of 'becoming known' was something that affected her chances of gaining tenure as well as opportunities for gaining employment in other universities. She spoke about how these connections affected the process by which 'becoming known' took place.

> In universities here in the US it feels like you have to have an advocate, someone who has the knowledge and the experience to point you in the right direction, someone who can tell you which conferences you should be going to and someone who can introduce you to the influential people. For many academics who are White, their circles are those which are attached to these kinds of networks, so they don't even have to try to make

an effort. They can just ask their senior colleagues, many of whom know others who can help them. But for those of us of colour, this becomes more difficult and so you have to work hard at it to ensure that the success you want can be achieved in that way (Black, female associate professor).

The idea of knowing the right people and having access to a 'network of knowns' was central to career progression, particularly in relation to improving one's curriculum vitae.

It is often hard for those people who do not have those connections to networks because it means that they have to work harder. But if you know someone who can help you, it means that they can point you in the right direction and make you feel that you are doing the right things and not wasting your time. If you do not have those connections, then a lot of the things that you do mean that you do end up wasting your time a lot and that obviously makes it harder (Black, female associate professor).

Others spoke about meeting the 'right people'.

I just happened to get introduced to Professor X who is well known and well liked in the field of Y. He is one person that seemed to have taken me on and really given me lots of opportunities to be able to move forward with my career and that means that he has introduced me to people who he knows and as a result I have been invited to present my work at international conferences and also I have been asked to chair panels that I would never have been able to do if I did not meet him and did not have that connection. His way of working is one that encourages those connections to happen and that has made a big difference to my career and how I will pursue certain avenues with my career (Black, female assistant professor).

One of the most successful forms of support that respondents spoke about was mentoring programmes.

Mentoring programmes

Many of the respondents spoke about the importance of formal and informal mentoring programmes and how they worked in the academy. Informal networks were considered by respondents as being the most effective. Formal mentoring programmes were important but were often related to universities 'ticking boxes' rather than meeting the needs of staff and were often directed towards junior or new members of staff. In some cases, the programmes consisted of individuals mentoring colleagues from different faculties.

78 *Understandings of identity in the academy*

Respondents felt that on the one hand, mentors were able to offer objective advice but on the other hand, some mentors did not understand the different ways in which certain faculties operated.

> We have several mentoring programs here, when I first started because I was a junior member of staff I was given a mentor who was in the same faculty as me and understood some of the issues and also some of my research areas. That worked in a great way because he had a vast amount of knowledge about the same areas as me, the same conferences and also the same sorts of funding applications I should be submitting. But then I had a new mentor who was from a different faculty and that did not work so well. But by that time I didn't need a mentor. Mentoring programs can work if your mentor knows about your research area and so can correctly advise you (Latina, female assistant professor).

Several respondents spoke about the timing of the mentoring programmes and how these worked in relation to their career trajectories. Some respondents felt that at certain points in their careers, they did not see the need for mentors, but they were keen to develop mentoring links with junior others.

> Once I had been promoted and gained my tenure, I knew that there was a limited value to having a mentor because I had gained knowledge and knew what to do with it. So I put myself forward for the mentoring programme to mentor others. I have found the mentoring to be very satisfying and have had the opportunity to mentor those who are similar to me – women of colour who understand the aspects of exclusion that women and people of colour face – and for many people that is a very important identifying factor that affects how one is seen and how one can move forward when thinking about different opportunities and making the most of them (Black, female distinguished professor).

Others spoke about how issues of identity made a difference to the mentoring experience.

> I think the situation is different for women and I wanted to ensure that I could mentor other women so that I could understand and empathise with their situation which meant I could provide them with better advice. For many women of colour their experiences are different to those of men of colour and they are seen to be disadvantaged in several ways. Another aspect that some of our junior colleagues talk about is childcare and how these different roles are juggled and of course this is not always the same for men, who do not have to think about these responsibilities (Black, female full professor).

Mentoring programmes and support networks were vital for Black African American academics to ensure their career progression as a source of information sharing.

Identity and intersectionalities of difference

Intersectionalities of identity played a key part in the experiences of Black African American academics and many suggested that their identities affected their chances of promotion and the opportunities that were available to them. One female academic spoke about the difficulties she encountered when she travelled overseas to attend conferences.

> I find it extremely stressful when I have to travel and leave my young children at home, they are safe and secure when I leave them and they are fine. But it is me and the expectations that I have for myself that makes me think I should not leave them. I ask myself if I am failing in my role as a mother and what does that mean for my role in the academy? The two roles are vastly different yet I know that being a mother is a much harder role. Black women of colour and women in general have to think about different factors that men do not have to think about (Black, female associate professor).

Female respondents spoke about how their experiences disadvantaged them compared to their male Black colleagues.

> I do feel that it is a little easier for Black men of colour than it is for Black women of colour. They are accepted into the academy in different ways to women and they don't have to deal with some of the overt sexism that exists in the academy at all levels. I am not naive in thinking that they still experience vast aspects of exclusion and racism but it is different for women of colour (Black, female assistant professor).

The different experiences of Black African men and women were also discussed in relation to the 'presentation of self'. Black women of colour felt that they had to develop a particular persona that would be accepted as being 'professional' in the academy.

> For many Black men of colour there is the pressure to look professional but that means they can wear a smart suit and a tie, but for Black women of colour it goes further than that. It's about ideas of sexuality and exoticism. You can be professional but you can't be sexy, you can be smart, but you can't be smarter than your White colleagues. And there are also degrees of acceptable standards and these are the unwritten rules (Black, female associate professor).

Whilst all Black African American academics experienced processes of racism, exclusion and marginalisation, these processes were understood by men and women differently and were often influenced by other identities such as gender and being a mother.

Educational leaders in the academy

Many of the respondents occupied senior leadership roles in the academy, yet they felt they had to constantly prove themselves to their White colleagues.

> I have taken on the role of departmental chair and although it is a role that many of us have to take on, it is also one that varies – depending on who is sitting in the chair. As a female person of colour, I know there have been instances when I have not been taken as seriously as White male colleagues when they are in this role. Sometimes, there is a constant questioning of you in that role. But I have used my power in such a way that I do not allow certain things to happen, and to some extent I use it in the same way as a White male colleague might. But because I am not White it is not seen in that way. I am sometimes seen as an angry Black woman, but that is my being assertive that is coming out (Black, female distinguished professor).

Black women of colour who were in positions of power and seniority often spoke about how their position and practices were compared to White, senior male academics. The identity and practices of White men was used as a measure from which judgements about the leadership skills of Black African American senior leaders were made. Consequently many Black women of colour struggled with their identity as senior leaders in the academy.

> As a Black woman of colour, I am often judged in comparison to the performance of White men. I should be judged on how I am performing my role as chair and not in comparison to how a White colleague performed his role as departmental chair a year ago (Black, female distinguished professor).

Whiteness was judged as the norm from which all other behaviour was defined. Respondents felt that universities operated on the basis that they were the preserve of the privileged few: those from White, male middle class backgrounds.

Strategies of success in the academy

Despite the challenges many of the respondents faced, they were able to use successful strategies in the academy to influence their career progressions. Some respondents spoke about the support they received from immediate

Understandings of identity in the academy 81

and extended family networks and colleagues at other universities. The central factor that was crucial for the support to be effective was based on the presence of an identity *with* those who provided the support as well as being a member of a similar organisation. These included religious and Black organisations, some of which operated via university networks.

> There are different strategies that I use in my life to ensure that I have the success that I need which will make a difference to my performance in the academy. The first and most important is the support that I get from my family and that includes my extended family. This support can work in different ways; it depends on what I need. Whilst my children are in day-care, there are other times that I may need that support and my parents and husband's family will always help out. This makes a difference to some of the decisions I make and some of the contributions I can make to my professional career (Black, female assistant professor).

Religious networks were also seen to be key strategies of support for some of the respondents. Many respondents spoke about their membership of religious churches which provided them with significant strength and reassurance when they felt they needed the support.

> I am a member of a church and I go to that church every week, but I am also connected to the church in other ways and we do lots of things for our community. All of the people in the church are professionals and we all recognise the difficulties we, as people of colour face in the academy and in the workplace in general. We talk about these things and we get strength from each other. We have even opened extra sessions for the Sunday School for the children, because we know about some of the prejudices that our children face in the schooling system. We cannot rely on others to provide that support so we support each other (Black, male full professor).

Another respondent spoke about a Black African American academics network which she had set up and which provided her with a great deal of support.

> A few years ago I was meeting the same people at conferences and we would go back to our respective universities and not have time to communicate and so I decided to set up an informal network. It means that we now meet properly when we are all at the same conferences and we can communicate through Facebook with each other. We can tell each other things that are going on and because we work in the same academic discipline there is a lot of overlap. This has developed in different ways and means that we have been able to support each other (Black, female full professor).

Several respondents spoke about this support as a sharing of experiences and identities.

> For me, it's about knowing that there are other Black women of colour out there who are also experiencing similar things to me. It's about knowing that I can speak to them about things and also that if I have an issue I can ask someone and that I am never stuck in any way. For me, the support doesn't have to be something concrete that I have written a paper with someone, it's about them being there for me in other ways. It's about providing emotional support and not feeling alone (Black, female assistant professor).

Support was instrumental, emotional and social. Whatever form the support took it was clearly something that respondents valued and many felt they could not do without.

> If I did not have that kind of support that I have from my family and also my networks I think things would be much harder for me than they are now. I would find it very difficult to progress and not be able to put things into perspective. Discussing issues with my family, my church or even my networks means that I can think of ways forward and share my issues (Black, male associate professor).

Respondents emphasised support as a two way process, particularly in relation to their religious affiliations and memberships.

> Many of us are members of our church and we think that we should all support each other. Part of this aspect is that we are members of the same community. So we look out for each other and look after each other and make sure that we support each other. We know that others do the same for their communities, so we have to do the same for our Black communities (Black, male associate professor).

The idea of belonging to a community with shared values was an important factor for respondents. Membership of a community enabled a mutual system and exchange of support to take place. Respondents relied on this support to help them to succeed in the White space of the academy.

This chapter has provided a critical understanding of race and identity within the context of higher education. It has specifically explored how BME academics are positioned in the academy and how their positioning is affected by aspects of gender, race, class and power. The chapter has drawn on empirical research to examine how identities are translated within the context of higher education and how BME academics understand their own identity within the context of higher education. The chapter has specifically focused on empirical data from respondents who were working in universities in the USA. The following chapter will explore the 'outsider' status of academics in the White space of the academy.

Note

1 Colour-blind ideology is a term used to refer to a practice which ignores racial characteristics in the selection of individuals.

References

Apple, M. (2006) *Educating the 'Right' Way: Markets, standards, God, and inequality*. New York: Routledge.

Aud, S., Hussar, W., Johnson, F. *et al*. (2012) *The Condition of Education 2012* (NCES 2012-045). U.S. Department of Education, National Centre for Education Statistics. Washington, DC. Available from: http://nces.ed.gov/pubsearch [Accessed: 23 May 2014].

Bass, L. and Faircloth, S. (2011) Female Faculty of Colour: Successful strategies in scademia. In Jean-Marie, G., and Lloyd-Jones, B. (eds) *Women of Color in Higher Education: Changing directions and new perspectives*. Boston, MA: Emerald Publishing Limited. pp.219–239.

Bennefield, R. (1990) Trench Warriors: On the front lines. *Black Issues in Higher Education*. 16, pp.69–71.

Bonilla-Silva, E. (2010) *Racism without Racists: Color- blind racism and the persistence of racial inequality in the United States*. Lanham, MD: Rowman and Littlefield.

Brown, D. (2003) Urban teachers' use of culturally responsive management strategies', *Theory into Practice*. Available from: http://www.findarticles.com/p/articles/mi_m0NQM/is_4_42/ai_111506823/print. [Accessed 30 May 2014].

Carpenter, B. and Diem, S. (2012) Re-thinking the preparation of educational leaders: Utilizing Q-methodology to facilitate the development of socially just leaders. In Boske, C. and Diem, S. (eds) *Global Leadership for Social Justice: Taking it from the field to practice*. Bingley, UK: Emerald Publishing Group, pp.43–57.

Diem, S. and Carpenter, B. (2013) Examining race-related silences: Interrogating the education of tomorrow's educational leaders. *Journal of Research in Leadership Education*. 8 (1), pp.56–76.

Diggs, G., Garrison-Wade, D., Estrada, D. and Galindo, R. (2009) Smiling faces and colored spaces: The experiences of faculty of color pursuing tenure in the academy. *Urban Review*. 41, pp.312–333.

Eagly, A. and Chin, J. (2010) Diversity and leadership in a changing world. *American Psychologist*. 65, pp.216–224.

Gallagher, A. and Trower, C. (2009) The demand for diversity. *The Chronicle of Higher Education*. Available from: http://chronicle.com/article/The-Demand-for-Diversity/44849 [Accessed 20 July 2014].

Gibson, S. (2006) Mentoring of women faculty: The role of organisational politics and culture. *Innovative Higher Education*. 3 (1), pp.63–79.

Habermas, J. (1998) Toward a critique of the theory of meaning. In Cooke, M. (ed) *On the Pragmatics of Communication*. Cambridge, MA: MIT Press, pp.277–306.

Hoyt, C. (2007) Women and leadership. In Norhouse, P. (ed) *Leadership: Theory and practice*. Thousand Oaks, CA: Sage Publications, pp.265–293.

Jackson, J. F. L. and O'Callaghan, E. (2009) What do we know about glass ceiling effects? A taxonomy and critical review to inform higher education research. *Research in Higher Education*. 50 pp.460–482.

Jean-Marie, G. (2010) Women's leadership in historically black colleges and universities. In O'Connor, K. and Greene, N. (eds) *Gender and Women's Leadership: A reference handbook*. Thousand Oaks, CA: Sage, pp.584–591.

Jean-Marie, G. and Brooks, J. (2011) Mentoring and supportive networks for women of colour in academe. In Jean-Marie, G., and Lloyd-Jones, B. (eds) *Women of Color in Higher Education: Changing directions and new perspectives*. Boston, MA: Emerald Publishing Limited, pp.91–108.

Jones, V. (2011) Building bridges for women of color in the professoriate. In Jean-Marie, G. and Lloyd-Jones, B. (eds) *Women of Color in Higher Education: Changing directions and new perspectives*. Boston, MA: Emerald Publishing Limited. pp.261–280.

Lester, J. (2008) Performing gender in the workplace: Gender socialisation, power and identity among women faculty. *Community College Review*. 34 (4), pp.277–305.

Lloyd-Jones, B. (2011) Examining the 'present' status of women of color. In Jean-Marie, G. and Lloyd-Jones, B. (eds) *Women of Color in Higher Education: Turbulent past, promising future*. Bingley, UK: Emerald Group Publishing, pp.1–28.

Madden, M. (2005) Gender and leadership in higher education. *Psychology of Women Quarterly*. 29 (1), pp.3–14.

Marcuse, H. (1968) *Essays in Critical Theory*. Oxford: Blackwell.

Mertz, N. (2011) Women of color faculty: Recruitment, hiring, and retention. In Jean-Marie, G. and Lloyd-Jones, B. (eds) *Diversity in Higher Education*. Bingley, UK: Emerald Publishers, pp.41–71.

Milner, H. (2010) *Culture, Curriculum, and Identity in Education*. New York: Palgrave Macmillan.

Mitchell, N. and Miller, J. (2011) The unwritten rules of the academy: A balancing act for women of colour. In Jean-Marie, G. and Lloyd-Jones, B. (eds) *Women of Color in Higher Education: Changing Directions and New Perspectives*. Bingley, UK: Emerald Group Publishing Limited, pp.193–218.

National Centre for Educational Statistics (NCES). (2009) *Projections of Educational Statistics to 2018*. Available from: http://nces.ed.gov/programs/digest/d09/tables/ [Accessed 13 April 2014].

Ropers-Huilman, B. (2008) Women faculty and the dance of identities: Constructing self and privilege within community. In Glazer-Raymo, J. (ed) *Unfinished Agendas: Women, gender, and the new challenges of higher education*. Baltimore, MD: Johns Hopkins University Press, pp.25–51.

Ryan, J. (2000) Educative leadership for culturally diverse schools. *Leading and Managing*. 6 (1), pp.1–20.

Ryan, J. (2003) *Leading Diverse Schools*. Dordrecht: Kluwer.

Sanchez-Hucles, J. and Sanchez, P. (2007) From margin to center: The voices of diverse feminist leaders. In Chin, C., Lott, B., Rice, J. and Sanchez-Hucles, J. (eds) *Women and Leadership*. Malden, MA: Blackwell, pp.209–227.

Sanchez-Hucles, J. and Davis, D. (2010) Women and women of color in leadership: Complexity, identity, and intersectionality. *American Psychological Review*. 65 (3), pp.171–181.

Schofield, J. (2010) International evidence on ability grouping with curriculum differentiation and the achievement gap in secondary schools. *Teachers College Record.* 112 (5), pp.1490–1526.

Seibert, S., Kraimer, M. and Liden, R. (2001) Social capital theory of career success. *Academy of Management Journal.* 44 (2), pp.219–237.

Theoharis, G. (2010) Disrupting injustice: Principals narrate the strategies they use to improve their schools and advance social justice. *Teachers College Record.* 112, pp.331–373.

Tooms, A., Lugg, C. and Bogatch, I. (2009) Rethinking the politics of fit and educational leadership. *Educational Administration Quarterly.* 46 (1), pp.96–129.

Turner, C. (2008) Women of color in academe: Experiences of the often invisible. In Glazer-Raymo, J. (ed) *Unfinished Agendas: New and continuing gender challenges in higher education.* Baltimore, MD: Johns Hopkins Press, pp.74–93.

Turner, C. and Myers, S. (2000) *Faculty of Color in Academe: Bittersweet success.* Boston, MA: Allyn & Bacon.

US Census Bureau. (2010) *Census Demographic Profiles.* Available from: http://2010.census.gov/2010censusu/data [Accessed 20 March 2014].

Uzzi, B. (1997) Toward a network perspective on organizational decline. *International Journal of Sociology and Social Policy.* 17 (7–8), pp.111–155.

Young, M. and Brooks, J. (2008) Supporting graduate students of color in educational administration preparation programmes. *Educational Administration Quarterly.* 44 (3), pp.391–423.

5 'Outsiders' in the academy?

This chapter will explore the 'outsider' status of BME academics in the White space of the academy. It will examine aspects of power, race, class and gender by comparing the experiences of BME academics in the UK and the USA. The chapter will conclude by analysing how a comparative perspective can provide an understanding of discourses of inclusion and equity for BME academics positioned as 'outsiders' in the academy.

Race and racism

Respondents were asked about their views on the study of race and racism in the academy. Many respondents were researching areas of race, diversity and inclusion in relation to social justice issues. Some expressed the view that because of their ethnicity, there was an assumption that they were *expected* to be interested in the subject of race and racism. Furthermore, they were also expected by their colleagues to take on roles which were related to diversity and equality issues, by virtue of their non-White identity.

All of the respondents talked about racism as a key factor in their experiences as BME academics in higher education. Racism for all of the respondents was seen as a factor that contributed to all aspects of their working lives: whether this was related to how they were treated by their White colleagues or students, the roles they were asked to perform or how they were judged in the academy. Furthermore, many spoke about how racism manifested itself in behaviour that was subtle, underlying and difficult to evidence. Whilst all universities had clear written equality policies, in reality it was difficult to explain how the policies worked in practice and their effectiveness in combatting racism and addressing inequalities in the academy. Furthermore, many felt that the claim by universities as being inclusive in their working practices was based on their portrayal of a positive external image, but in reality this was not the case.

Racism and racist bullying in UK higher education institutions

Many of the respondents spoke about their experiences of racist bullying. This behaviour was experienced from a variety of colleagues including line managers. Respondents felt they had to 'put up with it, because it was hard to prove'. Others decided to take action and tackle it head on by reporting it to their line managers, but in many instances they felt this was rarely taken seriously. Two respondents had made formal complaints about such behaviour, and another left their institution to seek new employment.

During the field work stage and the writing of this book, the preparation for Research Excellence Framework (REF) was taking place. The REF is the new system for assessing the quality of research in UK higher education institutions. The REF replaces the RAE (Research Assessment Exercise) which took place in 2008 and previous years. The process of the REF is managed by HEFCE (Higher Education Funding Council of England) and is overseen by the REF Steering group. The main aim of the REF is to assess outcomes for each higher education institution, based on their submissions. The assessment of outcomes will be used to inform the allocation of funding to higher education institutions. The REF is based on a process of expert review.[1]

The process of the REF has produced greater competition in the academy both within and between institutions. Many of the respondents spoke about the pressures of the REF creating greater competition between colleagues in individual departments. Consequently, this competitive edge was evidenced in the attitude of newly appointed colleagues who had joined departments. They had recently obtained their PhDs and regarded competition as part of the academy and their working lives. Many respondents mentioned pressures in the current economic and financial climate such as reduced budgets in university departments and the recent closures of several teacher training departments resulting in redundancies and greater pressure on those in employment to retain their jobs. Consequently, such an approach had fostered a 'culture of discontent' in the academy. Many academics spoke about battling to secure promotions and being entered for the REF and suggested that the culture in higher education was based on a 'dog eat dog' mentality and 'all for myself' attitude, which led to a decrease in collaboration, collegiality and support in many departments. Many referred to this as the 'ruthlessness' of the academy: an environment in which many were keen to climb the academic ladder of success without due regard for their colleagues. In such a climate, competition and the scarcity of jobs led to a persistence of incidents of racism and bullying.

All of the respondents spoke about how they had at some point in their academic careers experienced some form of overt or covert racism.

Many referred to how their colleagues made them *feel*; some respondents described this as a 'gut reaction' and behaviour that was difficult to prove. Farah, an Asian professor, expressed this as,

> It's subtle. It's not overt so you can't see it or prove it. You can't bring it out and challenge it. I am not sure it would be taken seriously anyway. If it's not tangible, then how do I challenge that? That is why we [ethnic minorities] have to be careful how we deal with our colleagues and their behaviour. We *know* that it's racism, we just *know* – but how can we prove it? How can we prove it if it's the small things like putting you down and undermining you – how can we attribute that behaviour to racism? We can't say *we know* it's racism, even though *it is* (original emphasis).

Tony, a Black Caribbean lecturer, was cautious when mentioning race as he felt his colleagues would assume that Black academics used their race as an advantage, for special treatment.

> If you talk about your race, it could be seen as special pleading which gives White people more ammunition against you. They may think you have a chip on your shoulder. People are polite to me, but at the same time they don't know how to take me so they are cautious around me. We [Black people] have to be careful that we are not accused of 'playing the race card' because then that means that racism and this kind of behaviour will just become devalued and seen as not being real or as not happening. There has to be a careful consideration about race and how it is used.

Tony described the overt and covert, subtle forms of racism he had experienced.

> They don't come and hit you over the head with a baseball bat and call you a [racist name], but they do other things that you know are based on race. Like excluding you from conversations by not asking your opinion which means they don't value what you have to say and don't want you to be part of the team. They do it by not giving you eye contact and not making you feel as though you are part of the group and that ultimately means your voice is not valued and not heard. That can be very frustrating and upsetting.

Many of the respondents spoke about how they were judged based on stereotypes of being Black or Asian. Tony, however, made a conscious effort to demonstrate behaviour that countered such stereotypes.

> As a Black male, it is important to be polite and professional at all times, more than it is for other males, because otherwise you will just get labelled as an aggressive male. White people will hold it against you

and think you are a stereotype confirming their views on Black people – aggressive and have a chip on your shoulder. So you have to be careful, you have to try and behave *against* the stereotype at all times and show that this is a stereotype and it is not the way that all people from one ethnic group behave. You have to *challenge* the stereotypes (original emphasis).

Martha's story

Martha described herself as Black Caribbean. She was a senior lecturer who worked in a 'new' university (post-1992). She had been working at her university for six years and during this time a new member of staff, a White middle class senior lecturer, also joined the department. Initially, Martha's relationship with John was professional and courteous until John began to line manage Martha. Martha described several incidents when John would openly criticise her in public; he would criticise her teaching, her administrative skills and her research. Martha began to feel she was being bullied as the behaviour continued over a period of time. After documenting the behaviour for a year, Martha decided to confront her manager. When she did so he was apologetic and denied any form of bullying. She told John that she was very upset by his persistent negative behaviour towards her and felt that it was a form of bullying.

> I felt that he would pick on me at any opportunity and make me feel worthless. He would treat me with contempt in public by putting me down. I felt that in return I had to just watch my back all the time and be careful because if I made a small mistake he would pick me up on it. He made me feel like I wasn't doing my job properly and so I lost all confidence and wanted to just leave but I couldn't leave without finding another job to go to. I did feel that it was racism and it was bullying, so I started to document what he way saying. I went to see someone in the union who suggested it might be racism. But racism is hard to prove if it is not obvious – and if you know and *feel* that it's racism how do you prove your case? (original emphasis).

Martha told John that she felt his behaviour was bullying, at which point he responded by telling her that she was exaggerating and did not have any evidence of this.

> He became quite worried I think when I said I felt that I was being discriminated against and he also realised that I was serious. Then when he knew that I didn't have anything concrete he did change his behaviour towards me, but it made me feel as though perhaps I was imagining it. When I spoke to the union they were very supportive but again said we needed concrete evidence to do something. I didn't actually use the

word and say to him [John] that it was racism because that would have been too much for him and for me – but I did say I felt it was discrimination of some kind. I think that surprised him as I think he thought I was the type of person who would not say anything or do anything about his behaviour towards me.

When Martha decided to report the behaviour to her head of department, the situation deteriorated.

> My head of department came across as though he didn't believe me; he couldn't understand that anyone in his department could be discriminatory or racist. He even suggested to me that I might be imagining it or thinking too much about it and it was just that me and John clashed as personalities. This made me very upset and also angry. I knew that if I didn't have the backing of my head of department I would have to just put up with the behaviour. I felt as though this is probably the way that many departments and managers deal with these issues of racism – if they come up. They must try and think they don't want this on their plates and so will do everything they can to say that it is something other than racism or discrimination – like a clash of personalities or something else – but to them they can't imagine it could ever be racism. They can't imagine that they could have someone who is racist in their department and this is the problem and this is where they are at fault. Racism and racists exist everywhere and in all walks of life – even in universities. That is something that many [White] people do not want to think about, because it puts them in the spotlight.

The situation deteriorated for Martha which resulted in her taking sick leave due to stress for several weeks. Martha finally left her university and found work at a junior grade as a lecturer in a different institution. She felt that she had jeopardised her career by taking a demotion and still feels upset about the experience.

> I think I should have stayed in the department and stuck it out. In the end I was pushed out because I didn't want to leave that university. But I had no choice because I was very unhappy. In some ways I have let John win the battle, so I feel disappointed about that but I am happier here. In the end, I couldn't cope with having to go to work and to think I had to see John and work with him. This was having an effect on my life and my family, it caused me a great deal of stress and I simply didn't think that it was worth staying there. It didn't take me very long to look for another job; it was easy in some ways because I was going from a senior lecturer to a lecturer grade. I do feel I made the correct decision but at the expense of risking my career progression. I have to wait to get promoted here to senior lecturer whereas in my previous university my next promotion would be principal lecturer.

John still works at the university and has subsequently been promoted to principal lecturer. Case studies such as this one about Martha are not unusual; I spoke to several respondents who had similar experiences, two of whom had taken their cases further to disciplinary action. But in all of the cases, there was no official recognition that the bullying behaviour was attributed to racism and discrimination which was the main cause of the problems. Respondents were told by senior managers that aspects of racism and discrimination were difficult to prove. Many respondents constantly referred to such behaviour as subtle and covert.

The positioning of BME academics in the UK

Many of the respondents spoke about how they were positioned as 'outsiders' in the academy, both by their colleagues and by structural processes in higher education. Peter a Black senior lecturer who worked in a research intensive university described his ethnicity which positioned him as an outsider.

> I think they respect me, but they could *fear* you. They don't want you to become uncooperative, so the fear might be what *appears* as respect or it is even closer to patronising at times. I'm not so sure how that works, whether they want you to feel as though they respect you *because* they want you to conform. They see me as a Black male and so I am judged because of that. Some of them see me as aggressive – but I would say I am not aggressive. They use their stereotypes of what they think about Black men and because they only use the stereotypes or perhaps have only those stereotypes to go on they are the ones who are often misplacing you because they don't know you. As a Black male it can be difficult at times and I don't want my behaviour to be misconstrued because some people can't separate their own prejudices from what is really going on in their institutions (original emphasis).

Other respondents spoke how they felt their colleagues *had* to respect them due to specific acceptable and non-acceptable behaviour that was allowed in universities. Paulette, a Black Caribbean senior lecturer, emphasised specific behaviour which had to be adhered to *because* it took place in the environment of the university.

> I don't think you can even know what your colleagues think about you, can you? Because they have to show some sort of professionalism and that means they have to treat you in a certain way. I do feel sometimes though that there are certain colleagues who resent my work and feel threatened by me and that comes across. But they have to continue to respect me – or they have to show they are doing that in public. Otherwise, they know we could always go to the policies [Equality Policy Committee] and say well I have not been treated equally like others have. There are certain ways in which people have to behave in the

> public arena of the university, but at the same time they don't have to behave like that anywhere else do they? We don't know how they behave in other public arenas or in their own homes. So it is difficult to know what is the real and genuine behaviour of your colleagues. They are aware of equalities policies and how they are *expected* to behave [original emphasis].

Farah (as previously), an Asian female professor, talked about how she had to constantly prove herself to members of her department, particularly her male colleagues.

> I feel I have to prove myself particularly with White men. There have been issues in the past where they do not respect my experience or what I have done. The other thing is, they seem to not see us as being individuals. For example, there is another Asian female in our department and people have confused us – which is strange because we look completely different – they have called me her name and vice versa. But they tend not to get White colleagues mixed up! The situation has become worse since I got my chair. I think some people just try and ignore me, but they do it in subtle ways and ways in which you know what they are doing but they try to hide their behaviour. They see me as being weak because I am a female and they see me as being someone who is not worthy of having a chair because I am Asian.

Many respondents also mentioned that their White colleagues did not expect them to respond to negative behaviour. If BME colleagues were criticised by their White colleagues, all said they would retaliate and defend themselves. However, when this happened, it was BME colleagues who were labelled as aggressive and defensive, as the following quotes demonstrate.

> I am often seen as being aggressive, but I am being assertive (Black, male senior lecturer).

> When White people are assertive this is seen as just that. But when Black people speak out, they are put into the category of having a chip on their shoulder and not being cooperative with their colleagues (Asian, female lecturer).

> I responded to an email that a colleague had sent which was in fact criticising me for doing something which I was not doing. The member of staff came to see me and said that *my emails to her* were aggressive and that I was aggressive in my manner. What she was really saying was, don't challenge me. But she turned it on to me, as though I was the one who had an issue. It seems that some colleagues think they can challenge you and that you are not able to defend yourself. But

if you are accusing me of something – and I have not done it – then I am definitely going to defend myself. It is this behaviour that I cannot understand. They [White colleagues] expect us to sit back and take the blame for things and not challenge them and when we do, we have the problem and the issue is with us and not them (original emphasis) (Black, female professor).

Jane, a professor, described herself as a Black African. She had been researching the area of race and racism for many years. She was a known figure in the area of race and racism in the academy and consequently felt in part accepted by the academy, but in other respects she felt she was an 'outsider'.

There's a sense of feeling that you don't belong here. In the academy race isn't at the forefront of people's agenda, it's on the outside of their experience so it gets difficult to discuss it, let alone for people to think about it. I don't think it registers on people's radar sometimes. I was at a meeting yesterday and colleagues were discussing social justice issues and it's funny really but people who claim to be fighting for social justice can make claims and not realise that *they* are continuing to stereotype and categorise – and be exclusive! I feel my work is respected only because I have received a lot of funding, and money matters, it is important. I am a professor and people know me and they know my work, but at the same time I also feel that my work is not respected because it is not seen as important as other areas are seen in my department, because it is race that I am interested in. I am also not convinced how much my colleagues would notice me or my work if I wasn't a professor or if I hadn't brought in large amounts of money. It's the big bucks that count.

Jane went on to say,

There are times when I feel like a member of the team and other times I feel like a Black member of the team.

Whiteness and Critical Race Theory

There has been a great deal of research which has explored the concept of Whiteness, particularly in relation to Critical Race Theory (CRT). Ladson-Billings (1998) states,

It is because of the value and meaning imputed to Whiteness that CRT becomes an important intellectual and social tool for deconstruction, reconstruction and construction; deconstruction of oppressive structures and discourses, reconstruction of human agency and construction of equitable and socially just relations of power.

(1998: 9)

CRT was first developed in the USA and grew out of the study of Critical Legal Studies which challenged traditional scholarship on legal and policy analysis. Kimberlé Crenshaw's work on Critical Legal Studies was influential in relation to the development of ideas on CRT. 'Critical Legal scholars have attempted to analyse legal ideology and discourses as a social artefact which operates to recreate and legitimate American society' (Crenshaw, 1988: 1350). CRT scholars work from the premise that racism is endemic in society (Delgado, 1995), and to demonstrate this they use storytelling to, 'analyse the myths, presuppositions and received wisdoms that make up the common culture about race and that invariably render Blacks and other minorities one down' (Delgado, 1995: xiv). CRT is also concerned with developing a critical standpoint to examine racism which suggests that White people have been the primary beneficiaries of legislation such as affirmative action in the USA (Guy-Sheftall, 1993). CRT also aims to give voice to those who are marginalised through the use of counter stories as a particular method of analysis, 'a counter story is needed to identify the desire for said communities for quality education despite mainstream accounts that depict communities of colour as 'anti-school' or 'anti-intellectual' (Stovall, 2006: 244).

CRT in the US and more recently in the UK has been used in educational analyses to explore how curriculum content (which is designed to maintain a White perspective) and stereotypes of the assessment of Black children are used to position them in schools (Gillborn, 2009). It has also been used to analyse how inequalities in school funding have contributed to institutional and structural racism and desegregation, processes which have been used to advantage the position of Whites and disadvantage the position of Black people (Ladson-Billings, 1998). 'For education, CRT is making attempts to confront White supremacy in the form of power of Whites in the school system and the resources that the majority wealthy White districts have and refuse to relinquish' (Stovall, 2006: 248). Solórzano and Yosso argue that CRT is crucial to explore how minorities remain marginalised and disadvantaged in education:

> CRT in education is defined as a framework or set of basic perspectives, methods and pedagogy that seeks to identify, analyse and transform those structural, cultural and interpersonal aspects of education that maintain the marginal position and subordination of African American and Latino scholars.
>
> (2000: 42)

David Gillborn has used CRT to examine educational policy making and its failings in the UK in relation to experiences of BME groups. 'Critical race theory promotes a different perspective on white supremacy than the limited and extreme understandings usually denoted by the term in everyday language' (2009: 56). He explores how racism has manifested itself in different ways in the making of educational policy making in the UK,

> race inequity and racism are central features of the education system. These are not aberrant nor accidental phenomena that will be ironed out in time, they are fundamental characteristics of the system. *It is in this sense that education policy is an act of white supremacy.*
>
> (2009: 63, original emphasis)

He goes on to state that, 'The evidence suggests that, despite a rhetoric of standards for all, education policy in England is actively involved in the defence, legitimation and extension of white supremacy' (2009: 65).

White researchers have also used CRT to challenge racism in education (Bergerson, 2003). Bergerson (2003) suggests that CRT scholars may oppose White researchers using CRT as this may demonstrate a form of colonisation in which White scholars will use CRT to promote their own interests and re-centre their own positions whilst attempting to represent the lives of people of colour. Bergerson uses CRT in her work by emphasising race as the main focal point of analysis and discussing liberal approaches to racism such as colour-blindness by placing an emphasis on the voices of people of colour as central to her analysis. 'Whiteness is a dominant transparent norm that defines what attributes of races should be counted, how to count them and who . . . gets to do the counting' (Mahoney, 1997: 314). The concept of Whiteness is one that is important because, 'White racism challenges the legitimacy of White people's lives' (Sleeter, 1994: 14). Bergerson recognises that,

> Whiteness is a race. The inability or unwillingness of Whites to see our Whiteness as a race is one of the most harmful aspects of supposed neutrality. Whiteness is neutral and all other colours are considered relative to Whiteness. In fact, if White as a race is taken into consideration it is impossible to ignore the privilege that comes with this race; the privilege to not think about race.
>
> (2003: 57)

Bergerson (2003) suggests that White researchers should attempt to use CRT in their work, but should do so strategically. 'Part of White privilege is the sense that Whiteness is normal or neutral. Centering race and seeing Whiteness as a race allows us to understand that White is not the neutral base from which all else is judged' (2003: 59). Leonardo (2002) has suggested that the study of Whiteness can be used to examine how White privilege has become institutionalised in all areas of society. Bush states that Whiteness, 'reveals the ways in which Whites benefit from a variety of institutional and social arrangements that often appear (to Whites) to have nothing to do with race' (2004: 15). Leonardo suggests that CRT itself is useful in explaining and analysing the inequalities in education attributed to racial differences.

> CRT is precisely that intervention that aims to halt racism by highlighting its pedagogical dimensions and affirming an equally pedagogical solution rooted in anti-racism. That said, CRT in education is a paradigmatic study of race to the extent that the problem of the color line is made to speak without a particular discourse, community and postulates... CRT focuses its attention on conceptual and practical strategies to end racism, less on ending race as an organising principle.
> (2009: 4)

In Leonardo's (2009) analysis of inequalities in education, he explores how White privilege and White racial hegemony works to enhance White supremacy, or indeed White racial domination. 'A critical pedagogy of White racial supremacy revolves less around the issue of unearned advantages, or the *state* of being dominant, and more direct processes that secure domination and the privileges associated with it' (2009: 75, original emphasis).

Some researchers have explored how the concept of multiculturalism can be used to challenge Whiteness and other forms of inequalities. Nieto states,

> Multicultural education is a process of comprehensive school reform and basic education for all students. It challenges and rejects racism and other forms of discrimination in schools and society and accepts and affirms the pluralism (ethnic, racial, linguistic, religious, economic and gender among others) that students, their communities and teachers reflect.
> (2000: 345)

Multiculturalism could be used to, '... potentially serve to challenge the dominant power structure in which access to resources, social awards and the power to shape the norms and values of society are afforded to those possessing White skin' (Jay, 2003: 6). It has also been argued that Whiteness and CRT can be used in teacher education programmes to explore the ways in which teachers themselves think about their own identities and how this impacts on their attitudes towards their own teaching.

> all teacher-preparation programs allow room for the study of Whiteness as it impacts teaching and teachers. Whiteness has been avoided in teacher preparation programs owing to the perceptions that it is either immaterial or dangerous. Rather than taking this approach, we suggest that Whiteness and White racism be introduced as a necessary component of any discussion of children and teachers.
> (Marx and Pennington, 2003: 106)

A significant number of respondents mentioned the identity of Whiteness when they spoke about their experiences of racism in the academy.

> There's a lot of bullying in the academy and there's a lot of racist bullying. Many of those at the top and even at the bottom can be dismissive of you and your work and patronising. So, there are always going to be victims and bullies. Many White people can and do use their sense of Whiteness and White privilege to bully a Black person. But this is done in a subtle way so that it can't be proved or stand up in an industrial tribunal (Black, female research assistant).

Respondents discussed Whiteness as having access to power and privilege. White people, *by virtue of their Whiteness*, occupied a position of power. Many of the respondents spoke about their position as marginalised 'outsiders' *in opposition to* the privileged position occupied by their White colleagues.

> White colleagues are in a position of power and privilege. They use that Whiteness – consciously or not – to further their careers. Some know that they have the privilege and use it, but others do so without knowing they have it. They are able to be considered for opportunities without having to ask about them. We have to push ourselves forward otherwise we get left behind. We are not White and so will always be judged as the outsiders, we will always be treated in a different way – often in negative ways – because we do not possess that identity of being White, of being privileged *because you are White* (original emphasis) (Black, female professor).

Many respondents mentioned that their White colleagues displayed a sense of privilege and entitlement to win large grants and publish in high status journals. When Black colleagues were successful in these activities, White colleagues displayed a sense of dissatisfaction indicating they should have been the ones who were successful in these areas.

> Some of my White colleagues behave very odd when I tell them that I am successful in something that I have achieved, whether that is a successful grant application or a piece of work that I have published. They seem to think I should not have it, but they should have it. I think this has to do with their Whiteness and their sense of entitlement. They cannot bear to think that we as Black academics have achieved something over them. Yet when they have achieved something, this is celebrated more widely by others than when we as Black academics achieve something. There is a sense that they are entitled to it because they are White, but we are not because we are Black (Black, male senior lecturer).

Being White was related to a sense of entitlement and privilege, a right to success. Black academics were constantly reminded by their White colleagues that they were 'outsiders' and by virtue of their Black identity would remain so.

Intersectionality and identity

The concept of intersectionality has been used to explore how different discourses of identity can be understood such as, for example, how race, gender, class, sexuality, age, disability and other axes of differentiation impact and define identities in various contexts (Collins, 2005). The concept has been used to analyse how identity can be explored as a dynamic rather than a static process, which changes at different times in different ways. Intersectionality is a model which engages with forms of difference in specific locations.

CRT is focused on exploring the impact of race and racism on education and how it works to marginalise Black people and their experiences. However, advocates of CRT also suggest that intersectionality is a useful concept that can be used and applied to understand these experiences. Bell suggests that,

> We emphasize our marginality and try to turn it toward advantageous perspective building and concrete advocacy on behalf of those oppressed by race and other interlocking factors of gender, economic class, and sexual orientation.
>
> (1995: 902)

From this perspective CRT and intersectionality have been used in their application to legal discourses and public policy. The work of Crenshaw (1989, 1991) addressed essentialist models of analyses by emphasising that a single analysis of race or gender did not explain or even acknowledge how Black women experienced their lives.

> Because of their intersectional identity as both women and of color within the discourses that are shaped to respond to one or the other, women of color are marginalized within both. . . . My focus on the intersections of race and gender only highlights the need to account for multiple grounds of identity when considering how the social world is constructed.
>
> (Crenshaw, 1991: 1243–1244)

Crenshaw's use of intersectionality through a legal framework argued against the use of a one-dimensional approach to understand Black women's experiences. Crenshaw suggests that,

'Outsiders' in the academy? 99

> The failure of feminism to interrogate race means that the resistance strategies of feminism will often replicate and reinforce the subordination of people of color, and the failure of antiracism to interrogate patriarchy means that antiracism will frequently reproduce the subordination of women.
>
> (Crenshaw, 1991: 1252)

The use of CRT in educational analyses has examined how race and racism operated in public education (Dixson, 2003) and the impact of race and gender on Black women's identities as teachers and student advocates (Dixson and Dingus, 2008). Others have used intersectionality to explore the experiences of Black male teachers (Lynn and Jennings, 2009).

In the UK discussions on intersectionality have focused on exploring how women defined their own identity in relation to being Black (Brah, 1996). Many of these discussions examined how essentialist assumptions of racism impacted on women's lives (such as through employment practices, domestic violence and the family) (Brah and Phoenix, 2004). The concept of intersectionality has received little attention in the UK compared to the USA. There has been little research which has explored how differences intersect and affect different forms of oppressions. Understandings of difference have been analysed as disparate entities and the study of race has been compartmentalised rather than being analysed in relation to other axes of difference such as class and gender (Bhopal, 2010). However some theorists such as Avtar Brah have used the concept of 'diaspora space' in her analysis of intersectionality to examine how identity changes in different historical locations and moments.

> Diaspora space is the intersectionality of diaspora, border and dis/location as a point of confluence of economic, political, cultural and psychic processes. It is where multiple subject positions are juxtaposed, contested, proclaimed or disavowed; where the permitted and the prohibited perpetually interrogate; and where the accepted and the transgressive imperceptibly mingle even while these syncretic forms may be disclaimed in the name of purity and tradition.
>
> (Brah, 1996: 208)

According to Brah, difference is conceptualised as part of a subjective experience based on location and space.

McCall (2005) however, has questioned the methodological frameworks used to analyse intersectionality. She suggests three different approaches for the study of intersectionality; anticategorical complexity, intercategorical complexity and intracategorical complexity. Nash's argument emphasises that, 'Intersectionality should explore difference, while also strategically mobilizing the language of commodity (however provisional or tentative that commonality might be) in the service of constructing a coherent theoretical and political agenda' (Nash, 2008: 4). Preston and Bhopal suggest the use of 'mash-up' theories in their analysis and use of interesectionality as ' . . . a productive way to consider the development of intersectional theorizing by not only examining what might be called the crossroads of personhood but also in terms of new theoretical integrations (or disintegrations)' (2011: 217). They suggest that theories of intersectionality should examine the White patriarchal structures in education and society more generally.

> The study of race and intersectionality is one where the production of new theory, to meet the complex worlds of the empirical is called for . . . as new theories are created, 'mashing up' traditional conceptions of 'race' and intersectionality, we should remember that theory in this area arose out of a direct challenge to White patriarchal structures in the academy and in wider society.
> (Preston and Bhopal, 2011: 219)

The following section will explore how intersectional identities affected how respondents were positioned in the academy.

Five respondents in the UK described themselves as mixed race. Two were from White/Asian backgrounds and three were from White/Black backgrounds. Two of the mixed race respondents (both female and from White/Asian backgrounds) described their mixed race as an advantage, related to their privileged middle class backgrounds. Parveen saw her mixed race identity as an advantage, she used her 'hidden identity' to conceal her true identity from her colleagues.

> As a mixed race person, I would say I occupy a privileged position because people don't know where I am from. They assume I must be White, but I am mixed White and Asian. They become surprised when I say that I celebrate things like Diwali because they see me as White. Whenever I show a marker of difference people are surprised and it is obvious that I am clearly middle class and because of that I am accepted more. My class appears to be more of an identifying factor than my race because visually I am very fair skinned and could be seen by my colleagues as being White.

Noreen emphasised that it was her gender that placed her in a disadvantaged position rather than her race. But equally she felt she was in a privileged position *because* of her mixed race identity because she could be seen by her colleagues as being either White or European.

> I would say it was my gender that has affected me here, because as a woman I feel I have to work harder. I don't think my ethnic background

or race comes into it to be honest. I am a woman first and a member of an ethnic minority second. For women, there are other things that we have to grapple with. I have heard colleagues make comments about women with children, about women who take maternity leave and women who have childcare responsibilities. It is mainly women without children who tend to be more critical about these things than men – which is very surprising. My sense is that gender is far more important than race and is far more discriminatory than race – because of having children and how women are seen.

Noreen described the colour of her skin as 'almost White'. It was this fair skinned identity which she felt enabled her to 'mingle in' with her White colleagues, consequently she did not feel discriminated against because of her racial or ethnic identity. Noreen was able to use her mixed race identity to 'pass as White' which she used as an advantage.

Shauna who also described herself as 'mixed heritage' was from a White/Asian background. She also felt her mixed race identity was an advantage, but felt discriminated against *because* of her identity.

I see my identity as a mixed heritage female as an advantage, lots of students can relate to me and they seek me out to find support from me. I think that's great because there is a direct connection that they have with me. If I can support them, then that is a good thing. But they don't go and do that to the White lecturers. I am seen as a hard worker and I get on with it, I don't think my race is an issue. If I was not such a hard worker then I think this may be attributed to my race, so they could have something to pin my incompetence on. I know the Black and mixed race students value my support. I feel placed, in some respects, by the students and not the institution. Also my research is not about race or racism and maybe that's why I am treated with respect by my colleagues. Not every Black or mixed race person needs to do research on race or teach about it. I actually think it's quite refreshing for White colleagues to meet a mixed race person *who isn't* researching race and inequality (original emphasis).

Noreen was reflective about her mixed heritage identity. She felt it affected how she was seen by the students, but she did not see this as being disadvantageous. She felt positioned by her students and not her colleagues and she attributed this to her *not* researching issues of race and racism or teaching these subjects.

I know there is always the assumption that if you are Black then you must be interested in studying race, ethnicity and diversity. But I have made a conscious decision not to study those areas. I am interested in them, but just because I am a mixed race woman does not mean that

> you can make that assumption that I want to study race. I have not sold out and I still identify with my Black background, but I choose not to study it and make it part of my professional career. Instead, I am more interested in the student as a learner and how they engage with their learning and what benefits them. This applies to all students and not just those from minority or ethnic backgrounds. My work covers *all students*, not just students who are from Black backgrounds and not just women students; it's about all students (original emphasis).

Jactina, also from a mixed race background (White/Asian), spoke about the intersectionalities of her identity, particularly in relation to her class background.

> I think my colleagues see me as having a Whiteness that is like them. I have a middle class accent, so people don't know how to pigeon hole me. There's a kind of reverse classism and racism going on – being of an acceptable class and race helps in the academy and can help you get promoted, because the university wants certain people to represent them and their image and who they are. They may see me like that because of the way I speak and so I am accepted, my background clearly comes through when I speak. Class has a greater impact in the academy in ways that I think we don't discuss anymore. We want to think that race is more important and that gender is more important, they are all important and need to be linked together. A working class Black woman will have a very different experience of the university than me – and that's because of the factors of being judged based on your class and your ethnic background.

Pauline, a Black Caribbean senior lecturer, emphasised how it was both her race and class that positioned her as an outsider.

> You don't operate on a level playing field with the rest of your colleagues. There is a sense that people tolerate you rather than accept you as an equal member of staff. It's very subtle. It's a feeling. Class has an awful lot to do with being excluded from certain discussions. I would say probably all of my colleagues are from middle class backgrounds. They all went to traditional universities and come from families which are clearly middle class. This is also the same for my Black colleagues. They have a certain kind of operating that they work in. It's difficult to explain, but I don't fit into it. That's my feeling. There are some Black colleagues who are able to fit in easier than me because of their accent and their connections. Being Black presents challenges, but being Black *and* working class presents greater challenges. If you're not in the crowd or around people who encourage you and guide you, you can become stuck. You won't have the best sources of information so that affects if you get ahead.

'Outsiders' in the academy? 103

Some (although very few) spoke about how their religious identity impacted on their positioning in the academy. Tariq, a Muslim senior lecturer, emphasised how his Muslim identity had a significant impact on how he was seen by his colleagues.

> As a Muslim man I feel that I'm probably treated a bit more hostile, with a bit more hostility than if I was a young Muslim woman. Conversely because I suspect that if I was a young Muslim woman I'd suffer greater disadvantage in society at large but maybe not in an academic environment. Because White liberal academics want to champion certain people, they like to have pet projects and I don't fall into that category. I fall into it because I'm brown, but I fall out of it because I'm Muslim. I kind of fall into it because I'm young, but fall out of it because I'm a man. My point is that White liberal academics can have the wrong prejudices, they want people to champion and promote but they prefer them to be non-threatening.

Tariq was very reflective about this own identity, particularly in relation to his religion. He made no efforts to hide his Muslim identity; instead he made a point of telling his colleagues that he was a Muslim.

> I think that some of them think I could be a radical Muslim who is into all sorts, but I am not. It's just that they don't know how to take me, when you say you are a Muslim people are immediately threatened by that. They expect you to hide your identity or not to be so open about it. But it is who I am and I don't think I should hide it.

The following sections will explore responses from respondents who worked in universities in the USA.

'Outsiders' in universities in the USA

Many respondents working in universities in the USA expressed similar views to those working in universities in the UK. The identity and privilege of Whiteness was something that many respondents in the USA referred to. They mentioned that the discourse of Whiteness was understood differently in the USA (given the history of race relations in the USA) and it was something that was openly discussed in the academy and in public discourse. Steven, a Black African full professor, expressed this as,

> We have a different history here to you in the UK, we have a history of slavery and there have been many instances of injustice and so we are more attuned to aspects of racism and we relate that to Whiteness and the development of Critical Race Theory has helped that understanding. There will always be an uneasy relationship between Black

and White people because we have the history and the understanding that being White automatically puts you in a position of power and ownership of White space – the academic space. As people of colour we have to grapple with these differences and how we tackle those differences depends on how we see ourselves. Some people of colour feel they are marginalised and do not feel as though they have any power to make any changes, others on the other hand see their Blackness as an expression of political power which can advocate change. I don't think it's understood in this way in the UK.

A significant number of respondents talked about the history of race relations in the USA and how this affected the positioning of Black people in USA society, as well as in the White space of the academy.

There is a lot of misunderstanding of Black people in the USA, there are many stereotypes around for example what a Black male looks like and how he behaves. There are aspects to do with masculinity, the dangerous Black man who has a heightened sexuality and also the gang member who will pull a gun on you. To some extent, these images are also taken into the academy and so we as Black men have to ensure that we do not conform to these stereotypes but are seen as Black brothers who are professional, well dressed and well spoken. Then we can move one step closer towards being accepted into the academy, if that is possible. So me and my brothers try and keep each other as allies in all places in the academy when we can do this because we know we are the ones who will be seen in a certain light and so we have to try and ensure that we are countering the stereotype (Black, male associate professor).

The idea of Blackness for male respondents was associated with Black masculinity and the stereotype of the 'dangerous Black male'. Black women on the other hand, had a different experience.

As a Black woman I know I have to dress well and be seen as professional and articulate so that I can be seen as part of the academy. I have been accepted in my position as a distinguished professor though I know that discrimination does exist and that I am seen differently from my White colleagues. I would say my position as a Black female has actually helped me to achieve my goals and has enabled me to progress further – as a Black woman with some power who can make a difference to the position of other Black women, who may not have that power. I think that may be different for Black males because they are often judged in relation to the stereotypes of Black men in the USA – and many academics do not know how to deal with them – because they use their stereotypes as signifiers of how certain people will behave (Black, female distinguished professor).

Julie discussed the existence of graduate and postgraduate courses which specifically focused on African American history and emphasised the importance of enabling Black academics to 'claim their place' in the White space of the academy. She related this to Black academics being able to display a sense of ownership and identity in relation to the subject matter in their teaching.

> We have a long tradition of teaching about the history of African Americans in the USA and there are many prestigious universities which teach these courses and so we are placed differently to our Black colleagues in the UK. As a result we have the reputation from our White colleagues because we have the academic backing. Even if our White colleagues don't want to acknowledge us, they have no choice but to acknowledge us. There are many high calibre universities which teach about Black African history and Black African studies so we have to be noticed and cannot be ignored. Because there are specific courses – and there are many of them – in prestigious universities then we are given the recognition that our history is one that is acknowledged and one that is worthy to be of intellectual importance – just like American History is. That intellectual space is one that can be claimed by people of colour in the USA (Black, female professor).

This historical association with an academic history that ensured Black academics were recognised was crucial in acknowledging the presence of a Black intellectual academic elite. Unlike the UK, the USA offered specific courses which explored Black African American history and contributed to how Black academics were positioned in universities in the USA and in public spaces.

> Of course we do have racism here in the USA and we have a history of racism and we will always have racism, we can't get away from that. We still have a long way to go, but because of the presence of the courses we have and also because there are greater numbers of Black faculty in universities, our White colleagues have to respect us – or at least appear to respect us. Discrimination does exist but it's perhaps not as overt as you have in the UK. Our White colleagues have to be careful here and treat us fairly. Our laws have a significant historical basis and they are taken seriously and all universities have to follow the rules. In general we are better in many respects than other employers. Also, universities and other employers don't want to do something that will put them in the news and spotlight so that they are seen as being racist or discriminatory. I would say we are more careful over here (Black, male professor).

Other respondents spoke about how their faculties actively recruited academics from Black or minority ethnic backgrounds and referred to this in relation to affirmative action. Affirmative action has a long history in the USA and refers to equal opportunity in employment practices. It was introduced to prevent discrimination against individuals on the grounds of their colour, religion, sex or national origin. The US Department of Labour has introduced different initiatives to target affirmative action such as the requirement for certain groups to have access to employment. This also includes specific support and outreach programmes for employees. The background to the introduction of affirmative action was based on historical disadvantages faced by minority groups as well as the need to ensure that public institutions such as schools and universities were representative of the wider population. However, affirmative action has been criticised for several reasons. Some educational polices on affirmative action which have quotas based on gender and race have been criticised as a form of reverse discrimination (Hurst, 2007). Consequently, some states in the USA have orders that do not allow discrimination and outlaw affirmative action regarding race, creed, colour religion, sexual orientation, nationality, gender, age and disability. Others such as California, Washington and Michigan prohibit affirmative action. The controversy regarding affirmative action is based on the notion that class inequality is more prevalent than other forms of inequality. Some have argued that affirmative action may benefit those from middle and upper class minority backgrounds at the expense of those from lower class and minority ethnic backgrounds (Sander, 2004).

Black identities

Many of the respondents working in universities in the USA spoke about their Black identity as a political identity; they referred to their ancestral history of slavery and oppression.

> As people of colour, as Black people we know about our history and we know what happened here in the US. There is a long history of Black slavery and oppression towards our people and it is something that haunts us. That is one of the reasons that we continue to fight for our cause, for our children and for the future. People of colour want equality and want to ensure that equality is translated into practice. It is something that our children are aware of when they go to school; it goes deeply here to the core more so than it does for other places and other people, probably more so than in the UK. We have a deep knowledge of how our history as Blacks has affected us and how slavery was something that has become part of our own identity as Black people. It is also part of what we understand in terms of the struggles of fighting for what we believe in and how we can progress from that. The idea of progress is important for future generations so that we can move ahead but also understand our history (Black, male professor).

Some respondents specifically emphasised that they used their own research as one of the ways in which they fought for social justice and equal rights for minority groups.

> One of the key components of being an academic is trying to make a difference in what you write and the research you do. My research on Black males in the classroom confirms that. As a Black man of colour I have to ensure that I am a successful role model and that I don't do anything that makes others think that I am like the stereotype of Black, aggressive men. I am able to do that through my work on social justice and equality and how that relates to the equity agenda. I can use that work to think about how it can be brought to the classroom to change stereotypes and to get White teachers to think about how their stereotypes will have an impact on young Black men of colour in the classroom (Black, male associate professor).

Many respondents were very proud of their Black identity and wanted to disprove the negative stereotypes that existed for Black men, and they did this by making a conscious effort to instigate change in educational practice.

> We have to continue to fight for our rights as people of colour. There is some understanding and also a narrative and discourse here that we have Obama, right? So we have tackled and resolved the issue of civil rights and equity campaigns so there's nothing more we need to do, right? But if you look deep down inside the schools, you see that African American kids are not performing well, there is a majority who live in the poorest areas and go to the worst public schools. They have little access to the advantages that some middle class people of colour have. So we have to continue to fight for those who are marginalised. Sometimes in our role as educators we think that the disadvantages can be explained by race alone, but it is more than that. Some of our Black children are living in the poorest and deprived areas of the city, their parents have no access to jobs and many of them are significantly disadvantaged because of those things. Income and class play a big part on the educational outcomes for Black children (Black, male associate professor).

Many respondents mentioned that the election of a Black president had influenced public and political discourses on race and equity in the academy and in society more generally.

> I think it has been positive for people of colour to have a Black president, but that has created a different way of thinking in that there is little recognition of discrimination now and the issue of affirmative action in some quarters is no longer taken as seriously as it once was. If we can have a Black African American president, then anything is possible, right?

How does that work? But we still have so many Black African American men who are unemployed and living on the breadline and so few going to college. It makes a mockery of the Civil rights movement. Of course it's a great historic moment that we have a Black president of the United States of America! But that greatness and advancement has to be translated into education and schools, by having a Black president doesn't mean we have simply solved every problem we have about race in this country (Black, male assistant professor).

Some female respondents emphasised how their experiences differed from those of Black men of colour in the academy.

As women of colour our experiences are not the same as Black men of colour. They have slightly better positive experiences than us and can manoeuvre in different circles compared to us, because they are men. We have to employ different strategies because many faculties at the most senior level are men – and they tend to be White men. But Black men of colour can try to fit into that level, but it is much harder for Black women of colour, we have different issues to negotiate such as sexism and how we are seen as being exotic and different because we are women and we are Black – there are particular stereotypes associated with that identity (Black, female assistant professor).

Some respondents also spoke about how their class identities played a major factor in how Black academics were positioned. Many were from middle and upper middle class backgrounds and the majority had come from backgrounds where education was valued and in many cases, their parents had been to university and/or were from professional backgrounds. A significant number of respondents felt that their class background enabled them to 'fit in' with their colleagues. Julia, a full professor, described this as,

If you are from a certain middle class background you are accepted into the academy. There are many different ways in which that can play out. Here we have fraternity and sorority houses and to be a member of those is based on your parents and your class background. Being a Black academic and being a well known distinguished professor I see that. But my class does make a difference to that and because I am seen as being middle or upper class because of my background and my status is advantageous for me. For other women of colour, if they are working class then they may not be so advantaged and they will be discriminated because of that. Class plays out more here than it probably does in the UK. Your class – and of course your race – can help to position you in the academy and in the way in which you are judged by society more generally. It is a powerful predictor of how you are judged and in education we know that it is a powerful predictor of educational outcome.

Julia described the existence of pay disparities between White and Black academics, as well as between male and female Black African Americans.

> There is data to suggest that Black African American male professors get paid more than Black African American female professors and that is widely known. So you have all sorts of disparities going on and it's hard to pin those down because the data that exists is either out dated or is confidential. But recently several universities have publicly said how much their employees earn and when we saw that, it was shocking to see not only the disparity between African American men and women, but also between Blacks and Whites – at similar grades. So where you think there may be equality – such as in being paid the same for the same job – may not necessarily be the case and you may be shocked to see that some of your colleagues – who may be junior than you, but are White – could be being paid the same or even more than you – that is a worrying fact.

Andrea, a Black assistant professor who defined herself from a working class background, was very aware of the class discrepancies that existed in the academy.

> Class has a lot to do with what is going on in universities. The universities tend to be focused around middle class norms and values and so they attract a certain sort of person that they want. There are different types of universities, but generally most of them are focused around what is middle class and the behaviours that entails. I noticed that when I became an academic because my background is not a traditional background. The more you are like them – like the others, mainly White academics in power – the more you will become accepted and class is part of that.

Many of the respondents also made a link between the class background of academics and the prestige associated with certain universities.

> You see that a lot of people who are at the elite, prestigious universities tend to be from upper and middle class backgrounds – if they are Black or White. Those universities do attract people from certain backgrounds and other universities tend to be more working class – this is not just for the academics, but also the students. The student body intake is one that is varied and mixed, but you see those students at elite universities are from affluent backgrounds – they would have to be able to afford the fees if they haven't won a scholarship, and that is also reflected in the staff body. Where you do have a mixture of Black and White staff, the Black staff are also from upper middle class backgrounds, yet they may be Black but they are still part of that elite group.

Some of the respondents who defined themselves as having a mixed race identity emphasised the importance of acknowledging and identifying with their Black racial heritage.

> As a mixed heritage female I consider myself Black and I would never want to be identified as White in any way at all. To me, that is saying that you are ashamed of your identity and not proud to be Black. I don't think many Black African American people of colour would do that here in the US. We see it as the 'one-drop rule', we as mixed heritage Americans would never be seen as White by society and society would not give us that label. We do not identify ourselves as being White. Instead, we identify ourselves as Black or mixed heritage (Mixed heritage, female assistant professor).

In the USA, the 'one-drop rule' (hypodescent) dates to a 1662 Virginia law on the treatment of mixed race individuals. The legal notion of hypodescent has been upheld as recently as 1985. The term was used to refer to the idea that any individual who has 'one drop of Negro blood' was considered Black. The idea of 'hypodescent' was based on the assignment of children from mixed parents to be assigned to the parent of Black ancestry. The one drop rule was not adopted as being a part of law until the twentieth century in Tennessee in 1910 and later in Virginia under the Racial Integrity Act of 1924. The one drop rule is controversial in the USA and different ethnic groups have their own ideas about its meaning and attribution. Many still consider those who are of a mixed heritage background as Black (unless they define themselves as White). However, the political ideas of the Black Power movement have been hugely influential in these definitions. They argue that those who have any African ancestry should define themselves as Black. Others have suggested that the one drop rule must consider the experiences, membership of communities and how individuals choose to define themselves (Powell, 2005).

This chapter has examined the position of BME academics in the academy. It has specifically explored the 'outsider' status of BME academics in the White space of the academy and examined aspects of power, race, class and gender by comparing the experiences of BME academics in the UK with those in the USA. The findings suggest that respondents from the UK and the USA have similar experiences of identity and positioning in the White space of the academy, but the political identity of being Black has different historical meanings for those from the USA. The following chapter will concentrate on the career progression of academics to provide a further understanding of racialised identities in the academy.

Note

1 http://www.ref.ac.uk/.

References

Bell, D. (1995) Who's afraid of critical race theory ? *University of Illinois Law Review.* 4, pp.893–910.

Bergerson, A. (2003) Critical race theory and white racism: Is there room for white scholars in fighting racism in education? *International Journal of Qualitative Studies in Education.* 16 (1), pp.51–63.

Bhopal, K. (2010) *Asian Women in Higher Education: Shared communities.* Stoke on Trent: Trentham.

Brah, A. (1996) *Cartographies of Diaspora: Contesting identities.* London: Sage.

Brah, A. and Phoenix, A. (2004) Ain't I a woman? Revisiting intersectionality. *Journal of International Women's Studies.* 5 (3), pp.75–86.

Bush, M. (2004) Race, ethnicity and whiteness. *Sage Race Relations Abstracts.* 29 (3), pp.5–48.

Collins, P. (2005) *Black Sexual Politics: African Americans, gender and the new racism.* New York: Routledge.

Crenshaw, K. (1988) Race, reform, and retrenchment: Transformation and legitimation in antidiscrimination law. *Harvard Law Review* pp.1331–87.

Crenshaw, K. (1989) Demarginalising the intersection of race and sex. *University of Chicago Legal Forum.* 140, pp.139–167.

Crenshaw, K. (1991) Mapping the margins: Intersectionality, identity politics, and violence against women of color. *Stanford Law Review.* 43 (6), pp.1241–1299.

Crenshaw, K. (2011) Twenty years of critical race theory: Looking back to move forward. *Connecticut Law Review.* 43 (5), pp.1253–1351.

Delgado, R. (1995) *Critical Race Theory: The cutting edge.* Philadelphia. PA: Temple University Press.

Dixson, A. (2003) 'LET'S DO THIS': Black Women preachers' politics and pedagogy. *Urban Education.* 38 (2), pp.217–235.

Dixson, A. and Dingus, J. (2008) In search of our mothers' gardens: Black women teachers and professional socialization. *Teachers College Record.* 110 (4), pp.805–837.

Gillborn, D. (2009) Education policy as an act of White supremacy: Whiteness, critical race theory and education reform. In Taylor, E., Gillborn, D. and Ladson-Billings, G. (eds) *Foundations of Critical Race Theory in Education.* London and New York: Routledge, pp.51–72.

Guy-Sheftall, B. (1993) *Black Feminist Perspectives on the Academy.* Paper presented to Annual American Educational Research Association Conference, 1993, Atlanta, April 13–15.

Hurst, C. (2007) *Social Inequality: Forms, causes and consequences.* Boston, MA: Pearson.

Jay, M. (2003) Critical race theory, multicultural education and the hidden curriculum of hegemony. *Multicultural Perspectives.* 5 (4), pp.3–9.

Ladson-Billings, G. (1998) Just what is critical race theory and what's it doing in a nice field like education? *International Journal of Qualitative Studies in Education.* 11 (1), pp.7–24.

Leonardo, Z. (2002) The souls of White folk: Critical pedagogy, whiteness studies and globalisation discourse. *Race, Ethnicity and Education.* 5 (1), pp.29–51.

Leonardo, Z. (2009) *Race, Whiteness and Education.* London and New York: Routledge.

Lynn, M. and Jennings, M. (2009) Power, politics, and critical race pedagogy: A critical race analysis of Black male teachers' pedagogy. *Race, Ethnicity and Education* 12 (2), pp.173–196.

Mahoney, M. (1997) The social construction of Whiteness. In Delgado, R. and Stefanic, J. (eds) *Critical White Studies: Looking behind the mirror*. Philadelphia, PA: Temple University Press, pp.310–333.

Marx, S. and Pennington, J. (2003) Pedagogies of critical race theory: Experimentations with White pre-service teachers. *Qualitative Studies in Education*. 16 (1), pp.91–110.

McCall, L. (2005) The complexity of intersectionality. *Signs: Journal of Women, Culture and. Society*. 30 (3), pp.1771–1800.

Nash, J. (2008) Rethinking intersectionality. *Feminist Review*. 89, pp.1–15.

Nieto, S. (2000) Teachers' experiences in a critical inquiry group: A conversation in three voices. *Teaching Education*. 13 (3), pp.341–355.

Powell, A. (2005) *'Passing' for Who You Really Are: Essays in support of multiracial whiteness*. Palm Coast, FL: Backintyme Publishing.

Preston, J. and Bhopal, K. (2011) Conclusion: Intersectional theories and 'race', from toolkit to 'mash-up'. In Bhopal, K. and Preston, J. (eds) *Intersectionality and 'Race' in Education*. London and New York: Routledge, pp.213–220.

Sander, R. (2004) A systematic analysis of affirmative action in law schools. *Stanford Law Review*. 57, pp.367–483.

Sleeter, C. (1994) White racism. *Multicultural Education*. 1, pp.5–39.

Solórzano, D. and Yosso, M. (2000) Critical race theory, racial micro aggressions, and campus racial climate: The experiences of African American college students. *The Journal of Negro Education*. 69 (1/2), pp.60–73.

Stovall, D. (2006) Forging community in race and class: Critical race theory, socialist critique, and the quest for social justice in education. *Race, Ethnicity and Education*. 9 (3), pp.243–260.

Web references

http://www.ref.ac.uk/. [Accessed 19 May 2014].

6 Climbing the ladder

Promotion and progression

This chapter will concentrate on the career progression of BME academics to provide an understanding of racialised identities in the academy. It will explore the discourses by which BME academics negotiate their identities in relation to their career progression and promotion. The chapter will examine the different facets and themes of identity within the context of belonging and exclusion within the academy and explore how these contribute to the 'outsider' status of BME academics in the White space of the academy.

Promotion and progression: UK respondents

All of the respondents spoke about their career progression and career trajectories and all mentioned the importance of promotion to senior positions such as senior lecturer, reader or professor. However, gaining promotion was not seen as a straight forward process of meeting specific criteria. Many felt it was based on 'being the right person', 'your face fitting in' and 'being in with the right people, those who have the power'. Many of the respondents were very committed to their jobs and all expressed a real desire to 'get on', but many emphasised that promotion was based on 'who you know', rather than 'what you know'. A mixed race Asian female senior lecturer said this was the case in her department.

> Universities are sort of incestuous; most of the people teaching are past students or sort of connected to the university. You see the same people, they go through the paperwork but jobs are tailored for these people and there is little room for real new comers. Getting a job is often based on who you know, and if you have worked in the organisation before and your face fits and they like you, you will be the one who is offered the job. Sometimes I wonder whether it's actually worth my time going through the process of applying for jobs and then asking colleagues to be referees because usually, departments know who they want to employ before the application goes in. Your networks provide you with greater power than your actual CV [curriculum vitae] does.

A Black female professor went on to elaborate.

> Being in the academy is about who and what you know. Despite having a lot of ambition, I have had no guidance on how to grow and nurture that ambition. In my department I was given lots of teaching but wanted to write and do more research. But I had to create my own opportunities and networks outside of the university, which made it very hard for me and placed me in a marginalised position. I think to some extent that has held me back, I know I should have got my chair way back but because I didn't know the things I should be doing and who I should be putting down as my referees that worked against me. I see other more junior colleagues in the same position and I think I am now in a position where I can help them and try to do that. As a Black female I won't have those connections compared to a White male who is more likely to have them.

Many of the respondents did not feel they were supported in their efforts to apply for promotion. They wanted to succeed, but were not given guidance on how to achieve this success. This lack of guidance was also linked to the 'glass ceiling effect'.

> There is a glass ceiling effect. Everyone at the top management and professors are White and middle class. There is a lack of transference of what to do to get there. I mean we could get guidance and support if we looked for it, but there is no available information on what we have to do to get there. In some sense, you could argue that there are deliberate mechanisms that may exclude us – as Black people – from those processes. We have to work it out ourselves and we have to ensure that we know what those processes are so that we can enable ourselves to get there. It's about who you know and who you relate to. You see some people – mostly White people – getting ahead than other people who work much harder than they [White people] do. I see it all the time (Black, female senior lecturer).

Many of the respondents spoke about this unfair treatment as a barrier to their promotion and progression. Some also saw this inequality when their departments appointed new members of staff.

> I have been on appointment panels and there have been good Black candidates and there have always been reasons why they have not been appointed. I find myself a lone voice fighting for them and speaking for them to be appointed. It's obvious that there's not massive numbers of Black candidates, but some of them we've had have been very good. But they just don't get appointed and that is a shame and it is worrying (Black, female professor).

Respondents who had served on selection panels discussed how the concept of 'potential' was often used to refer to a White candidate rather than a Black candidate. White candidates were more likely to be appointed due to their future potential – compared to BME candidates who had to demonstrate *actual* achievements.

Networks and contacts

Respondents in the USA explained the process of promotion and tenure as being fairer compared to that in the UK. Gaining tenure was based on a measurable system of criteria which consisted of presenting a portfolio of evidence and a narrative of work which outlined major achievements.

> We have a system here where you are not automatically granted tenure, instead you have to apply for your tenure and that can take a long time. It does mean that the system has specific criteria that you have to meet, but it also means that how you are viewed in the department can affect your chances of gaining tenure and who you choose as your reviewers. The objectivity stems from the availability of set criteria so you can go through the list and tick off what you have and ensure that you have a strong portfolio of evidence, but on the other hand when you select the reviewers it could be based on who you know. Also the whole process could be seen to be subjective because it is based on what the departmental chair and the committee think, and sometimes personal issues may come into that (Black, male associate professor).

Many respondents on both sides of the Atlantic expressed the notion that networks and contacts played a significant part in how careers were made. Having a network of established colleagues in senior positions was advantageous. In the USA this was recognised and acknowledged; there were Black people of colour in these positions who made a conscious effort to support junior colleagues who were from similar backgrounds to themselves.

> There are many senior Black faculty members here and many are distinguished or established professors who have been around for a long time and they know the ropes and they also know what you have to do to be accepted and to make a name for yourself. These Black senior people make an overt point of supporting junior colleagues and they do so with a view to encouraging them to become the next generation of scholars. Some of the things they are good at are to tell you which conferences you should go to, where you should publish your work and they also can offer to be your reviewers for your tenure. That kind of advice can make a very important difference to your career and how quickly you progress in your career (Black, male associate professor).

This explicit, 'looking after' of colleagues in the USA was something that many respondents referred to as a sense of duty to the next generation of Black scholars and to ensure a future representation of the Black academic elite.

> To think that there may not be a representation of Black academics for future generations would be very depressing. For that reason it is important that those in positions of power – like me – nurture and grow the next generation of academics. We have an academic elite here in the US and it must be preserved, but also it must include Black female and male academics who are part of that – otherwise we would no longer have that representation. So I use my position and influence to bring those younger Black academics along. If I can use my connections to help then, then I will do that. I am not doing anything that is different to what White academics do with their junior members of staff. They have been doing that kind of thing for generations (Black, male professor).

Martin a Black African American assistant professor benefitted from such mentoring.

> I would have no idea what to do if I did not have any support from the senior Black academics that I know. Some of them actively seek out more junior staff to support them. Their feeling is that, we have to look after our own because they know that racism exists here in the academy and White academics will not make efforts to encourage Black scholars. Of course, it does depend on where you are and which faculty you are in. But even in [name of subject] there is the tension around race and entitlement. I know that the support that I have received from some of my senior professors has had an impact on the advancement of my career.

Martin elaborated on the concept of entitlement.

> Many White colleagues do have a sense of entitlement, they feel it is their place to have and do things in the academy. Maybe it's because they see the academy as a traditionally White space and question whether we [Black people] have the right to be here. But it's also about the way that the entitlement works. If you as a Black male have something that you have achieved, there's a distinct feeling as though you should not have it and you should be grateful if you do. There is some sense of resentment from White colleagues when you have something and they don't. They make you feel as though the space is not for you, but for them. This is something that is a historically Black USA thing, because it goes back to slavery and equal rights. We are historically seen

as slaves without any rights and certainly not to be in positions of power and so some White people interpret this as *their* sense of entitlement. And we have it, it is *theirs* not ours [original emphasis].

Many of the UK respondents also expressed similar views. Janice, a Black lecturer from the UK, said,

> There is not that much support here in terms of career progression. For instance other Black senior colleagues may not necessarily seek you out to support you. That is something that you have to do yourself and most are quite accommodating, but in the end the types of networks that you are associated with determine your success and if you are a Black person or from a minority ethnic group then that means it is often harder for you to access those groups.

Becky who was from the UK had struggled to become a professor and felt that she wanted to actively support her colleagues because she knew how difficult it was to gain promotion and to gain a sense of credibility in her field of education and in academia.

> I realise the difficulty of gaining promotion and getting that superiority so that you are taken seriously and knowing that your White colleagues do value your work. It is very difficult to achieve this and sometimes it means you have to go out of your way to support your Black junior colleagues otherwise they would not progress. It's the same strategies that White colleagues use to support others. We have to realise that these issues play a big part in the academic community and some people for whatever reason or another are unable to make those significant links.

Respondents in the UK and the USA recognised the importance of networking and support from those in senior academic positions. Networking and support from senior colleagues played a key role in career progression and promotion.

Researching race, diversity and inclusion

Many of the respondents were researching issues to do with race, diversity and inclusion. Those who were studying race felt that such a topic was judged by many of their White colleagues as 'personal research', research that was about them and their own lives, others felt they had to apologise for studying race and some did not feel valued because they studied race. As Farida, an Asian professor from the UK, said,

> Race is devalued as a study in academia because it is Black people who study race. There are some White people who study race, but their

> work on race is valued more because they are White. So they [Black people] are not seen as suitable for some positions in the academy. I didn't start out researching race, but when I did I noticed how my work became less important and devalued. A lot of us [Black people] do make that decision that we want to study race and make it our area of specialism, but I think at the same time we have to be careful that we are not judged because of that. Most of the time we are judged because of that and because we are Black and because there is little value attached to our research. We are not felt to be worthy and our research is not taken seriously.

Some respondents said several universities did not value research which focused on race and equity. Patrick, a Black lecturer who worked in a research intensive university in the UK, said,

> Being in a leading research intensive university, there are some subjects in my department that are more valued than others. I do feel isolated in my research. It is not recognised as being worthy; I would say it is overtly marginalised. It is not considered to be as important as other research, but I know colleagues who are working in 'new' [post-1992] universities in similar areas where their research is more valued and given greater prominence than mine is here. I feel that is related to what the university thinks is important and how they want to translate that to the outside face of the university.

Others spoke about their areas of research not being 'acceptable enough' and 'too risky to support' because it was seen as 'controversial and questioning the status quo' in the academy.

> I don't do research on the right areas to get promoted. Race is not respected, so if you choose to work in this area you won't get promoted. You just get marginalised and side-lined. Race is not seen as important or worthy as other topics. There are mostly Black colleagues who work in the area of race equality or inclusion, so when we say certain things these are not respected. But what is interesting is when a non BME academic who may be in a senior position says the same things, they are taken seriously. But I do think there is more kudos and respect attached to a statement about racism in society and in the social structures that is taken on board if it is said by a White person than if it is said by a BME person (Asian, female professor).

A few respondents felt it was important to have 'White allies' in the academy.

> I think it's really important to have people speaking on behalf of us [as Black people] because if they are the ones who can say certain things

and be accepted for it, it means that those things are still said even though we [as Black people] have not said them. We need White people to be our allies; it makes a difference to how our work is seen and what it means to us (Asian, female senior lecturer).

Some respondents on the other hand disagreed with having 'White allies'.

I do get annoyed when White Europeans stand up and wave the race flag and talk about racism – how could they possibly empathise and how could they possibly understand how it makes *us* [Black people] feel? [original emphasis] (Black, male senior lecturer).

There's a lot of intellectual typecasting that goes on in the academy. As an ethnic minority you are *expected* to work on minority ethnic issues, it's like if you're not then there is something wrong with you. That's one of my bug bears – because not all of my work is in that area, so there is an assumption that I do not take it serious because I am not doing research on it. But then you have White academics who do the same sort of work but *because they are White* it is seen differently and taken far more seriously [original emphasis] (Black, male research assistant).

Many of the respondents felt that researching areas such as race, diversity and inclusion was seen as 'personal research' by their White colleagues.

Role models

All of the respondents spoke about being a role model for students and the effect this had on their academic careers. Respondents saw this as a positive aspect of their work, particularly for those who felt that they could influence the experiences and careers of Black students. Respondents from the UK expressed this as an important part of their job which they greatly valued.

Being a role model for all students should be an important part of our job, but being a role model for Black students is very satisfying for me. I am able to support them in many different ways. Lots of them come to me and tell me that they value me and my work. I can see that they seek me out because they want that identity of similarity, as I am able to understand their feelings and sometimes their feelings of being isolated. They also look to me and think that they too could also do this job – which many of them see as a middle class profession which is linked to social class – so it is important that they see us [as Black people] and know that this is also a profession that is open to them (Black, female professor).

Other respondents did not want Black students to feel marginalised in the academy and went to great efforts to support them.

> Many of the Black students sometimes feel out of place here, because perhaps their parents didn't go to university. So I feel in my role as a Black academic I should be supporting them and helping them to achieve what they can. They look to me to be a role model and I am conscious of that so I try and support them as much as I can (Black, male professor).

Some respondents spoke about how Black students actively sought their support – over and beyond their White colleagues.

> I know that a lot of the Black students come and find me and want to see me and want me to help them with their work and I am happy to do that, but at the same time I know it works the other way. Some of the White students do not respect me sometimes and I feel they may be also seeking out the White lecturers to get support from them, so we have to be careful how that works. It may be the same thing with the White students, they may think that I am unable to support them or cannot identify with them because I am Black – so they go to the White academics (Black, female senior lecturer).

Respondents also said that students wanted Black academics to be positive role models for them.

> Lots of the students say that I am a role model for them and that makes my job worthwhile. I feel that I have achieved something when I help students and am able to support them. They often tell me that they like it that they have someone who is like them to look up to and to be able to know that they can achieve as well. This is more so for the postgraduate students because they feel that they too could have a career in the academy despite its downfalls (Black, female professor).

Many of the respondents in the USA also felt that part of the success of their job was being a positive role model for their students.

> Over here [in the USA], there is this stereotype that there are not enough Black positive role models for boys, so as a Black male of colour I think it is my duty to be a positive role model for them. They come from backgrounds where their parents may not have gone to university themselves and so we can step in and support them when they feel they need the support. I feel that is part of my role as a Black male and I feel that it should be part of my role (Black, male associate professor).

Respondents in both the UK and the USA reported being a role model for Black students as a positive experience which was a satisfying aspect of their job.

Identities and routes to promotion

Many of the female respondents felt that their Black ethnic identity affected whether they would be considered for promotion. Mary, a Black Caribbean who had recently been promoted to a professor in a 'new' (post-1992) university in the UK, said,

> I think there is a definite disadvantage to being a woman and a Black woman. Because a typical university is dominated by White men. If you're a woman you have to work harder. If you're a Black woman you have to work three or even four times harder. If you're working class, this will also go against you so you have several obstacles that you have to manage. I think it's more about race than gender to be honest. Women have come on a lot I think. It has to do more with race. In the psyche the idea of being Black and being a professor don't match do they? And there is a huge problem of acceptance that comes with that. I feel much more accepted overseas than I do here. For example when I go to the States, I feel much more respected and feel that my work is taken more seriously over there than here. And also, there is a critical mass of people that I can identify with and work with.

Some also spoke about their roles as mothers in the academy.

> We have a glass ceiling, but it's also about the structures in place which disadvantage minority people. The structures don't allow us to get promoted. For example as a woman with children I am disadvantaged because of the things I can and can't do and as a Black woman that is judged more harshly than it would be for a White woman – who is seen more sympathetically than me (Black, female senior lecturer).

Other respondents in the UK mentioned the identity and privilege of Whiteness that existed in the academy and how this worked to disadvantage those from BME backgrounds.

> The custom and practice of universities is to maintain a White environment. So people do not get treated the same, some are treated well and others are not. It's important that staff are supported in their career progression, there should be mentoring programmes to enable staff to do this. Universities should also review their recruitment policies and look at ways in which they can attract more Black staff. More open dialogue is needed with staff to do this, but they are reluctant to do this as

they want to maintain the White superiority and the Whiteness of the institution (Black, male senior lecturer).

Another respondent related the issue of Whiteness to how racism was understood in the academy.

> You have to be careful when you talk about race and racism because if you bring it up or keep bringing it up they [White colleagues] think you are the one who has the problem, when really they don't want to confront their own issues of White privilege and how they can use their Whiteness as a form of power. But you can *never* use your identity as a form of power. If you ever mention race and racism, you would be seen as having a chip on your shoulder and that is often the stereotype of all Black people [original emphasis] (Black, male research assistant).

Some of the respondents spoke about how they were positioned in the academy in relation to their gender and class and how this related to their opportunities for promotion. Class was seen as a powerful and significant determinant of how one's position in the academy was viewed.

> I think social class intersects more with race and gender because it determines how people see you and how they ultimately define you. But it's more difficult to pin that connection down sometimes. For example I know I have a strong middle class accent and my social class is an advantage and I know that. If I am honest, I would say I use that more as an advantage than my race because my race is not an advantage (Mixed race, female senior lecturer).

Many of respondents felt that their race, gender and class had a significant impact on how they were seen by their students, their colleagues and their chances of promotion and progression in the academy.

Power

Some of the respondents spoke about how certain credentials not often possessed by BME academics were valuable in the academy. Nahir, a Muslim senior lecturer working in the UK, said,

> The academy is a very cut throat business, it is very competitive and can grind you down and make you feel like a failure. You need to know who the power brokers are, and as Black person you don't know who they are or how they work. You are not part of their gang. As an academic you're inevitably caught in that tangled web. Also, there's a degree of rhetorical legitimacy that accompanies your success in the academia. If I were to bring a million pounds next month, I would be viewed

radically differently because as much as a certain type of intellectual currency is valuable, it is not nearly as valuable as monetary currency.

Power also manifested itself in other ways. Many respondents felt that White colleagues could define levels of professional practice in the academy and how they operated.

> I have to be careful because as a Black person White colleagues expect you to be perfect in everything. If you make a mistake they are quick to jump on it but they don't do that to other White colleagues. If I make a very small mistake it is noticed, yet there are White colleagues who are not doing things well and are making mistakes all the time – but they don't get told off or pulled up about it. It seems one rule for White colleagues and another rule for Black colleagues. Yet, if you were to say that to colleagues I think they would be horrified that you could think such a thing – so I don't know how this type of racism works. But it is indirect and subtle. That is why it is difficult to prove. It is how institutional racism is defined; it is part of the structure (Black, female professor).

Many of the BME respondents in the UK said that they felt BME colleagues had to work much harder than their White colleagues to receive recognition from their department and to get promoted. Some also felt marginalised in their departments because they did not feel that their work was valued.

> I've had to be two or three times better than other colleagues to get my promotion. I did get it in the end, but other colleagues who didn't have as much as me such as publications and money have got promoted. Ethnic minorities have to be much better to be promoted and even then they might not get it. It is more about ethnicity than gender. You do have White women in senior positions in universities, but you don't have Black women and you don't have Black vice chancellors. So there must be something that's not quite right out there (Black, female professor).

Another Black, female senior lecturer said,

> My ethnicity, class and gender have all affected my chances of promotion. The problem with these experiences however, is that they can leave one feeling responsible. So even knowing that these elements have played a crucial role in my career development, I'm forced to ask myself if I've been – at least practically – to blame. You know, perhaps if I'd have been better prepared, better organised, more demanding and more active in exploring possibilities – then maybe things could have been different for me.

Some of the respondents blamed themselves for their lack of success and not pursuing networks which could have contributed to their promotion and career progression. Others suggested that it was important to build networks of support which existed outside of their own universities.

> It's important to build your networks outside of the university and to make connections with others working in your area so that you can get support from them. Work on race is not respected, the journals you write in are not seen as important as other journals and your work is just not seen to be significant. Black academics continue to be marginalised (Black, male lecturer).

Others felt that some departments displayed their understanding of inclusion and diversity by the presence of 'just one' Black academic in their department.

> Some universities have one Black person in the department, so you become the acceptable face of that department. So they can then say, yes we are inclusive, look we have employed a Black person [laughs]. That is often what happens in many mainly White departments, they have to have one person because otherwise it may look suspicious that they have not employed any Black academics in their departments. I think departments do this and know that they are doing it. Having one Black person could signify that you have ticked the diversity box (Black male, research assistant).

Whilst many respondents felt that universities operated an inclusive agenda, they indicated that this was not reflected in practice.

> I don't know how it works, whether senior managers sit round a table and actually say things – or whether it comes out in certain ways. For example shortlisting candidates and how that might work they could just shortlist people who are like them – and they are White and are in positions of power – so they shortlist other White people. So it could be happening on an unconscious level. But it's hard to tell (Asian, male senior lecturer).

There were several factors that respondents discussed in relation to their positioning in the academy and how this affected their chances of promotion. Their different identities clearly played an important part in this.

Credibility

Many respondents in the UK discussed the notion of 'credibility' and how this worked in their departments. This concept was spoken about but rarely defined and many respondents felt it was based on trust.

> I want to take on more senior roles in the department but I am not sure I have the credibility or whether people will think that I will be able to lead the department. I think that has to do with my race and also my gender, because I am a Black woman from a working class background I will be treated differently to how a White man from a middle class background will be seen. I have already seen how I am treated by the students and the staff as well. They do not give me the same amount of respect and do not listen to the things that I am saying compared to how they treat White male senior colleagues. I am told that credibility is very important, but I am never told what it actually means? (Black, female senior lecturer).

The idea of trust was related to the over scrutiny of colleagues. Many respondents raised the issue that their credibility was questioned from their colleagues. For instance some respondents referred to this in relation to their colleagues questioning whether they had published a particular paper in a leading journal, whether they were the lead author on a paper or whether their publication was in a 'real book'.

> I remember being questioned about my work and whether I had in fact had all those publications, because they are all in top journals. I was also asked whether I really was the lead author as well because my work has been recognised by top universities and top journals. The idea that it couldn't be my work is insulting and I don't think a White male colleague would be asked that question (Asian, female senior lecturer).

Another respondent added,

> I think when you have a successful book published by a prestigious publisher, some of my White colleagues were quite shocked that I had got that contract and that I was the lead author. It's almost as if they can't believe that I am capable of writing or publishing for a prestigious publisher. They feel that it should be theirs, by rights, and not ours. Even though we have worked very hard to get what we have achieved. They have no idea how hard we have worked and how many attempts it has taken us – they just see the end product and assume it has been easy (Black, female professor).

Respondents also spoke about the higher threshold that was raised for them compared to their White colleagues. The higher threshold was one that was related to promotion and progression in which respondents felt they would be judged differently compared to their White colleagues. Black colleagues felt they were often asked to show a track record of achievements rather than potential, which was not the case for White colleagues.

> We have to show clear evidence that we have achieved everything when we want to go for a more senior management role, but for others it is not really like that. They can show that they have the potential to succeed and to go further. We are not allowed to do that, we have to show that we have done everything and have it all in front of us (Black, male senior lecturer).

Others spoke about not having a 'buffer'; a form of support or someone they could rely on – something they said that their White colleagues had.

> I do not have buffers and I can't rely on them. I know that if I make a mistake then I would lose my job and it would be gone. Compared to other people, mainly my White colleagues they would be given the benefit of doubt and they have the buffers that they can rely on. Also, if you have buffers you also have the power. You know that someone is supporting you. But it's very different for us [Black academics] (Black, female professor).

Support was considered a vital factor for all respondents.

> The kind of support you receive from your colleagues is very important, it determines how far you can go in the academy and it also determines what you end up doing. It determines where you publish and what you achieve. I can see a lot of my White colleagues who have that support and who are able to have more opportunities given to them than I would ever have (Asian, female senior lecturer).

Many of the respondents in the USA also expressed similar views. All of the respondents were very ambitious and wanted to achieve their full tenure or full professorships. Yet they also felt they had little support, few buffers and had to find support from similar colleagues (such as those who were also Black people of colour). Many also indicated that the support they received was from their colleagues who were outside of their own institutions.

> Support is important, but sometimes there are too many issues going on in departments so you have to seek support elsewhere, outside of your institution. I find that I can get that kind of support from those who are not working with me, and they are able to give me good advice which will help me further. I also think that we should be mentoring others too. If we are in positions of authority then we should use that as an advantage and take it forward to be supportive to others who may need it (Black, female associate professor).

The process of tenure in the USA was one that was fraught with challenges and difficulties for those respondents who had not yet achieved it. Many were nervous about having to apply for tenure and others also expressed the fear that they may not achieve it.

> It is always hard going for tenure, because you never know what the outcome is going to be and it is so important and you need to be successful. If you don't get it in one place it can go against you and it can affect your reputation. It can have a big impact on your career and where you see your future in terms of your career and your future in faculties (Black, male assistant professor).

There was a clear indication from respondents in the USA that there were discrepancies in the process. A few of the respondents spoke about this in terms of a meritocracy.

> I think the system of tenure and full professorship is unfair. There are criteria to be met, but there are also those underlying prejudices that are hard to pin down. There are many people of colour who do not get their full professorships and they struggle. These are Black colleagues who have succeeded and have incredible reputations, but they still don't have their full professorships and so you wonder why that is so. The idea of a meritocracy is good in theory but it doesn't happen in practice. If we lived in a true meritocracy then we would all have achieved our full tenure professor positions. But getting that full professorship is not about meritocracy it is about more than that (Black, male associate professor).

The idea that success was based on connections and networks – other than significant achievements was something that was mentioned by many respondents.

> There are some universities which are very prestigious and they operate to keep them a certain way. I would not say that was that they want them to be White; I would say it is more to do with class. There are plenty of very middle class Black African Americans who are part of that club. Class is more important here. If you are a member of the privileged class and you are affluent then you can still go to the Harvard and Yale if you are Black (Black, female professor).

The idea of being part of a privileged class was not only confined to those who were White.

> Class plays a big part here. Most the top Black African American professors tend to be from middle or even upper class backgrounds, though not all. If you are working class and a person of colour then it is harder, there are more obstacles in your way. It is possible but harder (Black, male associate professor).

There was also a feeling that the culture of elite universities was one that reproduced middle class values and norms which were represented in the types of individuals who were employed in such universities.

> There is also the notion that the prestigious universities are keen to keep themselves represented as they are. They occupy a privileged position and want to keep that position as well as their status in the league tables so they will do what they can to do that. So for some people of colour it is harder for them to get into those institutions, both as students and as professors (Black, female assistant professor).

Another respondent commented,

> In the UK the idea of keeping certain institutions as elite and in positions of power is to enable them to stay as they are. So the elite universities have few students and staff from minority ethnic backgrounds and so they maintain their elite status by keeping the status quo. Keeping institutions being able to manifest certain kind of culture and also so that a certain kind of student and academic applies to those institutions is essential to maintain their status quo (Black, male assistant professor).

Many of the respondents from both the UK and the USA were adamant that the elite universities would continue to maintain their elite status by *not* admitting those from working class or Black minority ethnic backgrounds. Consequently, the idea of inequality and discrimination was something that many of the respondents discussed in relation to this. This discrimination was described as subtle and covert, existing at all structural levels and affecting students and staff – but manifesting itself in different ways. This chapter has examined respondents' views on progression and promotion in the academy. The following chapter will explore how BME identities in the academy can be understood in relation to aspects of inclusion, equity and social justice.

7 Inclusion, equality and social justice

This chapter will explore how BME identities in the academy are understood in relation to inclusion, equity and social justice.

Understanding diversity in the USA

There are a variety of diversity and equity programmes that have historically existed in the USA. These include affirmative action, diversity committees and taskforces, diversity managers, diversity training, networking programmes and mentoring programmes. Kalev et al. (2006: 590) state that, 'Each of these programs may well increase diversity . . . our contribution is to show that organisational structures allocating responsibility for change may be more effective than programs targeting either managerial bias or the social isolation of disadvantaged groups'. Whilst there is evidence to suggest a decrease in gender and ethnic inequalities in the workforce, there is little evidence to suggest that this may be a direct result of diversity programmes (Tomaskovic-Devey et al., 2006). Tomaskovic-Devey et al. suggest that reasons for this may be because,

> structures establishing responsibility (affirmative action plans, diversity committees and diversity staff positions) are followed by significant increases in managerial diversity. Programs that target managerial stereotyping through education and feedback (diversity training and diversity evaluations) are not followed by increases in diversity.
>
> (2006: 590)

Furthermore, when diversity programmes are introduced in organisations, managers do not always see it as their responsibility to instigate them, or as their responsibility to promote greater gender and racial equality which can contribute to a social justice and inclusive agenda in the workplace (Reskin, 2003). Kalev et al. (2006), however, are optimistic in their approach to diversity programmes and suggest that there are certain measures that can be taken to ensure that workplaces are dealing with aspects of diversity, for example the assignment of specific roles to individuals who take responsibility for setting an agenda based on equity and achieving specific goals of diversity. This can also include different models in which progress for diversity can be measured by joined up thinking in organisations. They also suggest that specific committees dedicated to the progress of diversity in which individuals are employed specifically for these purposes would be beneficial to ensure that diversity is taken seriously in an organisation, and consequently measured and acted upon.

Others have suggested that diversity training can have negative effects on employees such as increasing rather than decreasing prejudice in the workplace (Kidder et al., 2004); or minority groups may benefit from reverse discrimination because of it (Taylor, 1995). It could also instigate negative reactions to minority colleagues in which others may seem them, 'as attempting to obtain power by individual and collective means' (Ragins, 1995: 106). However, some research has suggested that organisational structures can make a difference to diversity, particularly when personnel systems are formalised to reduce favouritism against particular groups (Reskin and McBrier, 2000). Others have been more critical of inclusive measures and suggest that employers may use practices such as anti-discrimination measures, simply as a means to defend themselves in court (Edelman et al., 2001). Kalev et al. state, 'Our findings suggest that although inequality in attainment at work may be rooted in managerial bias and the social isolation of women and minorities, the best hope for remedying it may lie in practices that assign organisational responsibility for change' (2006: 611).

Strachan et al. (2007) point out that the concept 'managing diversity' has been used in diversity and equality forums in the USA and Australia. Legally, there has been a great deal of pressure on organisations to address aspects of diversity in the labour market and this has resulted in the use of different perspectives in management and implementation diversity. Some have suggested that the concept of 'managing diversity' is an alternative to focusing on affirmative action which may be regarded as a process of solving discrimination (Agocs and Burr, 1996). Agocs and Burr state,

> organisations are dealing with diversity in their client and customer populations as well as among their employees. Responding effectively to a more heterogeneous customer base is a requirement in the growing service sector ... moreover workforce diversity presents a challenge to organisations that are devolving a variety of responsibilities to decision-making teams, which increasingly consist of individuals of varying backgrounds.
>
> (1996: 31)

They also argue that managing diversity can be seen as a positive step forward for staff retention and can increase the career development of minority groups who continue to be disadvantaged in the labour market. However, there are many different mechanisms in place for 'managing diversity' in the workplace. Bartz et al. (1990: 321) suggest that managing diversity should include, ' . . . understanding that there are differences among employees and that these differences, if properly managed, are an asset to work being carried out more efficiently and effectively'. Indeed such differences need to be taken into consideration when diversity and inclusion are emphasised as practices in organisations. Others have suggested that managing diversity should emphasise opportunity for all members of the workforce to fulfil their potential and 'is founded on the premise that harnessing these differences will create a productive environment in which everybody feels valued, where their talents are being fully utilised in which organisational gaols are met' (Kandola and Fullerton, 1994: 8). Gill (1996), however, suggests that managing diversity should be understood in relation to how equal opportunities can be achieved in which all individuals are given the chance to excel in the workplace.

Inequality and diversity in the workplace

Some researchers have demonstrated that diversity training can increase rather than decrease bias and prejudice towards particular groups in the workplace (Kidder et al., 2004). For example, Thomas (2001) suggests that White men are more likely to benefit from the creation and working of networking and social ties in the workplace compared to their Black colleagues. Whilst social networks have shown to be beneficial for individuals in the workplace, particularly in relation to promotion and progression, it is Black men who are disadvantaged in this process.

Studies have explored the effects of diversity on racism in the workplace. Bonilla-Silva and Forman (2000) suggest new ways of analysing racism in which Whites use 'a new *racetalk* to avoid 'appearing' racist and that the themes and arguments that they mobilise are congruent with what other analyses have labelled as 'laissez-faire' or 'competitive' racism' (Bonilla-Silva and Forman, 2000: 50, original emphasis). Bonilla-Silva and Forman (2000) suggest that there has been a change in the way in which racism is understood and expressed in the USA.

> We believe . . . that there has been a rearticulation of the dominant racial themes (less *overt* expression of racial resentment about issues in the Jim Crow era such as strict racial segregation in schools, neighbourhoods and social life in general), and more resentment on new issues such as affirmative action, government intervention and welfare and . . . a new way of talking about racial issues in public venues – a new racetalk – has emerged. Nonetheless the new racial ideology continues to help in the reproduction of White supremacy.
>
> (2000: 52, original emphasis)

Bonilla-Silva and Forman's (2000) research study showed that respondents were more likely to display racist views in their interviews than in their survey responses. 'The apparent discursive contradictions and hesitations were *resolved* by turning liberalism into an *abstract* matter' (Bonilla-Silva and Forman, 2000: 77, original emphasis). White respondents justified their own views by blaming Blacks for their position in society. 'Whites resolutely deny that racial inequality is structural and second, they explain it as the result of Blacks' "cultural deficiency" (e.g. they are lazy, their families are in shambles and their communities are bursting with crime)' (2000: 77–78). The research suggests that whilst respondents agree that Black people experience racism and discrimination, these are the views of a minority. Other respondents in the study suggested that Black people used racism and discrimination as an excuse to explain their failures in society. Black communities were judged as the 'other'.

> Specifically they construe Blacks as culturally inferior; as living in a tangle of pathology. Thus, not surprisingly, most of our White respondents blamed Blacks themselves for their lower status. At best, the respondents felt pity for Blacks, at worst many openly expressed contempt and hostility towards Blacks.
>
> (2000: 78)

Bonilla-Silva and Forman argue that this type of colour-blind racism is justified by Whites, ' . . . the liberal free market and pragmatic rhetoric of colour-blind racism allows Whites to defend White supremacy in an apparently non-racial manner' (2000: 78; see also Bobo and Hutchings, 1996). The authors argue that the concept of colour-blind racism justifies the views of racists by appearing not to be racist because the racism they express is not overt,

> Colour blind racism allows Whites to appear 'not racist', preserve their privileged status, blame Blacks for their lower status and criticise any institutional approach – such as affirmative action – that attempts to ameliorate racial inequality . . . we must unmask colour-blind racists by showing how their views, arguments and lifestyles are (White) colour-coded. We must also show how their colour-blind rationales defend systemic White privilege.
>
> (2000: 78)

Understanding diversity in the UK

Much of the legislation on diversity and equality in the UK has been geared towards solving problems and complaints rather than employers showing a commitment to diversity and equity in their organisations (Wilson and

Iles, 1999). The research has focused on how diversity programmes are managed in relation to outcomes and how diversity affects the organisational structure (Easley, 2001). Deem and Morley (2006) suggest that there have been changes in the ways in which diversity is understood in higher education institutions in the UK, resulting in an auditing and managing culture. An increase in student diversity has provided the basis for a focus on diversity in higher education, rather than an exploration of what diversity means for the staff body and the workforce. Consequently, institutions have a greater focus on their student intake rather than their staff. Deem and Morley's research suggests that,

> equality for staff as compared with students does not seem to lie at the heart of higher education's management priorities. Many staff interviewed thought of equality issues, if they considered them at all, as bound up with identity and choice and not the material conditions of existence and there was widespread belief that student equality is a higher institutional priority than staff equality.
> (2006: 197)

Social justice and inclusion in education

Early research on inclusion in the UK focused on examining the marginalisation of those who were defined as having special educational needs in the education system. This perspective did not examine how such groups were marginalised due to the structural processes of the educational system. Fulcher states, '... it is a failure in the education apparatus by those whose concern it should be to provide an inclusive curriculum and to provide teachers with a sense of competence in such a curriculum, which constructs the politics of integration' (1989: 276). The UNESCO *Ensuring Access to Education for All* policy focuses on how inclusion can contribute to creating a more socially just society by providing access to education for all groups in society (UNESCO, 2005). The *Salamanca Statement* (UNESCO, 1994) emphasised that all children have the right to an education regardless of their individual circumstances. It is based on a Framework for Action which emphasises the needs of the child as the central focus in relation to providing children with adequate teaching and learning in schools. The *World Declaration on Education for All* (EFA) programme was adopted as a result of the Jomtien conference in 1990. This model is based on a transformation of attitudes and values towards inclusion in which education can be used to transform the lives of those who remain marginalised in society.

The Warnock Report, which was published in the UK in 1978, outlined how special educational needs could be understood within a macro perspective. Some suggest that the Warnock Report did not fulfil its aims of exploring how special educational needs could be understood from such a perspective.

> Ultimately the Warnock Report's approach to special education failed. In part, this was because it put forward a definition of special education needs without any clear principles to guide resource allocation. More specifically it failed because its philosophy was grounded in a post-war model of welfarism that was about to be superseded by the neo-liberal philosophy of personal choices as the driving force for making schools and teachers accountable for educational outcomes of their pupils.
>
> (Armstrong et al., 2010: 24)

Armstrong et al. (2010) also state that many governments have been concerned about inclusion in policy making decisions but these have focused on, '... technical approaches to inclusive education that framed those policy applications in the UK in the narrower terms of school improvement, diversity or provision for different needs and academic achievement' (Armstrong et al., 2010: 6).

The concept of inclusion has been discussed at great length and there are many different discourses that attempt to analyse its application in educational settings (Barton, 1998). Ainscow et al. (2006) discuss two different types of inclusive approaches: descriptive and prescriptive. Descriptive inclusion refers to how inclusion works in practice and prescriptive inclusion refers to how the concept is used. They also argue that there are 'narrow' and 'broad' definitions of inclusion, with narrow definitions referring to the focus on a specific group and broad definitions which explore a diverse range of groups. Discussions on inclusion have led to the development of the Index for Inclusion (Ainscow et al., 2006) which is based on the development of a set of indicators that can be used to examine how a consideration of aspects of inclusion can be used when schools refer to inclusion and diversity. Such concepts include 'respect for diversity', aspects of 'community' and 'equity', 'participation', 'compassion' and sustainability'. In order for inclusion to take place, Ainscow et al. (2006) suggest that schools have to understand inclusion as a dynamic rather than a static process. Leo and Barton (2006) have suggested that inclusion can only take place in schools if senior managers are aware that inclusion can be used to instigate change in schools. Ainscow et al. (2006) suggest a typology for exploring how educational practitioners can think about inclusion in order for it to happen:

> as a concern with disabled students and those categorised as 'having special educational needs'; as a response to disciplinary exclusion; in relation to all groups as being vulnerable to exclusion; as developing the school for all pupils; as 'Education for All'; as a principled approach to education and society.
>
> (Ainscow et al., 2006: 15)

They suggest that,

> Inclusion is concerned with all children and young people in schools; it is focused on presence, participation and achievement; inclusion and exclusion are linked together such that inclusion involves the active combating of exclusion; and inclusion is seen as a never-ending process. Thus an inclusive school is one that is on the move, rather than one that has reached a perfect state.
>
> (Ainscow et al., 2006: 25)

Inclusion in the USA

Apple (2013) argues that in order for inclusion to take place in society, we must explore how education can be used as a signifier for change, particularly for marginalised and oppressed groups. With increasing instability and insecurity in society, it is educators who have a crucial role to play in the inclusion of marginalised groups. Apple's emphasis on political change and activism is one which explores how practical changes can make a difference to those who remain marginalised in educational structures.

> Challenging these economic, social, cultural/ideological, and affective structures and relations asks us to work on many lives and in many sites. We all have roles to play in this process. Some roles will be historical and conceptual. Some will involve working directly with students in critical ways.
>
> (Apple, 2013: 166)

In order for education to be effective and instigate change, educators must work collectively to ensure that education can affect and change the lives of those who remain marginalised. Apple suggests that the personal has to be political,

> among the tasks of the critical scholar/activist in education is to continually and publicly recognise the importance of such hard ideological and personal work and to be even more open to learning from multiple critical traditions. One cannot adequately answer the question of whether education can change society unless one looks at society from the position of *multiple* oppressed groups.
>
> (2013: 12, original emphasis)

Other researchers have explored how aspects of multicultural education can affect social justice and equity in education programmes. Grant and Sleeter (2007) outline how incorporating multicultural perspectives into everyday teaching can contribute to providing an inclusive education for students, at all stages of their educational careers. They argue that in order for this to take place students from diverse backgrounds have to be taught by teachers who are aware of the individual differences that a diverse range of students bring to the classroom. Nieto (2003) emphasises that teachers must be committed to inclusive teaching methods to understand the experiences of those from marginalised backgrounds. McCombs states that, 'student's perceptions that their teacher's learner-centred classroom practices are the most significant predictors of student motivation and achievement' (2003: 96). Schultz (2003) suggests that one of the ways that this can happen is by developing a framework for listening to students and considering their individual characteristics and how these can contribute to greater inclusive teaching methods, which will benefit all students and teachers.

Social justice in the USA

The literature in the USA which has explored aspects of social justice has examined how teachers define and understand social justice in relation to their own practices in the classroom. Some researchers have suggested that White, middle class teachers need to think about their own attitudes and beliefs towards students of colour and those from marginalised backgrounds and how this affects their teaching perspectives (Grant, 1994; Banks, 1995; Ladson-Billings, 1995).

The work of Marion Young (1990) has explored how social relations and processes affect group differences in the process of marginalisation. Young argues that in order to explore social justice and how it can be addressed, we must explore the role of social relations and how individuals interact in such situations. As members of different social groups with different attributes, it is these relationships that we must think about in relation to aspects of social justice. 'Where social group differences exist and some groups are privileged while others are oppressed, social justice requires explicitly acknowledging and attending to those group differences in order to undermine oppression' (Young, 1990: 3). This takes place through a process of respecting group differences without re-establishing forms of different oppression. 'This definition suggests that social justice teacher education provides prospective teachers with opportunities to develop respect for individual differences and recognise how those differences might be informed by the individual's affiliations with particular social groups, such as those based on race, ethnicity or class' (McDonald, 2005: 422). McDonald (2005) argues that in order to think about how social justice operates in the classroom, there are certain questions that have to be considered such as, 'Do teachers' opportunities in courses tend to emphasise one dimension of social justice – a focus on individual needs for example – over others. What opportunities do teachers have to appropriate both conceptual and practical tools related to each dimension of social justice?' (2005: 432). Others have suggested that it is approaches to multicultural education that have contributed to aspects of social justice and inclusion in the classroom, particularly in relation to racial and other differences (Sleeter and Grant, 1987; Nieto, 2000). Nieto (2000), for example, suggests that all schools should consider how teacher education programmes can be inclusive, 'to take a stand on social justice and diversity; make social justice ubiquitous in teacher education and promote teaching as a lifelong journey of transformation' (2000: 192–183). Using a social justice lens can also influence how teachers think about and relate to students from diverse backgrounds (Cochran-Smith, 1997). Nagda et al. (2003) suggest that multicultural education can be used to explore how educational transformation can take place in the classroom, particularly in relation to addressing those who remain marginalised and excluded. This has become ever more apparent in challenging institutional racism in schools (Sleeter, 1996). Nieto (2000) suggests that in order for teachers to challenge institutional racism in the classroom, they must develop a critical emancipatory and anti-oppressive approach to pedagogy. Nagda et al. state, 'While coming from different epistemological foundations, the focus of both multicultural education and critical pedagogy is to analyse social life through a lens of diversity and social justice and to prepare students to be transformative democratic agents' (2003: 167). Aspects of social justice should also explore curriculum content which can focus on achieving equality and social justice in the classroom and in doing so, challenge the dominant power relationships that exist in society (Sleeter, 1996). Ethnically diverse teachers in classrooms can enhance the academic and social experiences of students of colour by using their experiences to serve as cultural mediators (Ladson-Billings, 1992). Sleeter (1993) argues that such a situation can also help to reduce the potential for discrimination against those from minority backgrounds. However, Sleeter and Grant (2003) suggest that whilst it is important to create a safe and secure environment in which aspects of social justice can take place in the classroom, there is some reluctance from White teachers to engage and work with those from poor and marginalised backgrounds. Montecinos and Rios in their study (1999: 73) found that the majority of the ethnically diverse teachers who participated saw schools as more than simply places to teach and to learn: they can be instrumental in improving conditions for the community. They also emphasise the importance of cultural awareness in the classroom which has a positive effect on all students including an appreciation for and the provision of a culturally responsive curriculum.

Banks (2007) on the other hand asserts that whilst social justice and inclusive education is possible, the focus must be on exploring the possibilities and challenges of educating students for citizenship in a pluralistic democratic society. He suggests that those focusing on providing a multicultural education for all students should focus on, ' . . . reforming schools to make them more democratic and to increase their capacity to educate students from diverse backgrounds to become thoughtful and active citizens' (2007: xi). In order for students to become effective citizens, students need to develop reflective identifications with their community culture, the nation-state and with the global community. In the past, schools in democratic societies tried to help students become effective citizens of the nation-state by alienating them from their community cultures and languages.

(2007: xiv)

Banks argues that citizenship education, '... needs to be changed in significant ways because of the increasing diversity within nation-states throughout the world and the quests by racial, ethnic, cultural and religious groups for cultural recognition and rights' (2007: 154). Other researchers, however, have suggested that in order for social justice and equity to be achieved, there is a need to explore differences in access to education such as parental income and socio-economic status which may serve to further marginalise minority groups, particularly in relation to access to higher education in the USA (Bowen et al., 2009).

Identity and inclusion

There is a great deal of research which has explored how Whiteness operates in the classroom as a form of privilege (Rodriguez, 2000; Leonardo, 2002). The study of Whiteness has been used to analyse how teachers understand their own racial identity and how this affects their classroom practice and interactions with their students (Sleeter, 1993). 'Teacher education must help candidates understand their own racial identity formation and provide the learning space to work with a range of emotions and feelings of indignation that evolve from an exposure to White privilege and the "myth of meritocracy"' (Solomon et al., 2005: 147). Solomon et al. argue that those in power are able to construct discourses, 'that are academically and emotionally debilitating to the "racial other". Such construction and related action is informed by a White, race-privileged position' (2005: 147). Solomon et al. also state that teachers often deny the existence of their own White privilege, '... another reaction to the notion of White privilege was that some of the teacher candidates in the study attempted to deny the existence of White privilege and its attendant capital and material benefits' (2005: 157).

Many researchers have explored aspects of Whiteness in relation to micro aggressions (Solórzano et al., 2000). These are described as subtle forms of racism which are often pervasive and work to marginalise people of colour (Delgado and Stefanic, 1992). Lorde (1992) and Marable (1992) suggest that racism includes aspects of institutional power which people of colour are less likely to possess than Whites. Solórzano et al. state, 'Indeed it is typically in subtle and covert ways (i.e. private conversations) that racism manifests itself. These innocuous forms of racist behaviour constitute racial micro aggressions' (2000: 61). Others have used Critical Race Theory (CRT) to explain how racism works to disadvantage people of colour particularly in relation to education (Ladson-Billings and Tate, 1995). CRT works on several premises; race and intersectionality are central to the focus of analysis; a challenge of the dominant ideologies through an understanding that people of colour are treated as marginalised in society and a commitment to issues of social justice and equity for people of colour.

> The Critical Race Theory framework for education is different from other CRT frameworks because it simultaneously attempts to foreground race and racism in the research as well as challenge the traditional paradigms, methods, texts and separate discourses on race, gender and class by showing how these social constructs intersect to impact on communities of colour.
> (Solórzano et al., 2000: 63)

The following sections of the chapter will explore empirical data which specifically focuses on aspects of diversity, inclusion and social justice in the UK.

Diversity and equity in the UK

Many of the respondents spoke about diversity in their own organisations, both in terms of student intake and the numbers of staff who were from BME backgrounds. Many respondents who were working at 'new' (post-1992) universities indicated that the student intake was often very diverse – consisting of students from Black, Asian and mixed heritage backgrounds as well as those from White and other backgrounds. However, whilst this was often the case there was also an indication that staff diversity did not represent the student body. Even when universities were located in areas with high numbers of BME individuals in the population, the staff body did not necessarily represent this. In some cases, respondents discussed the widening participation agenda in relation to universities actively encouraging an agenda to increase student diversity (such as those from disadvantaged and marginalised backgrounds), but emphasised that this was not the case for the staff body. The widening participation agenda is based on a commitment by HEFCE (Higher Education Funding Council of England) and OFFA (Office for Fair Access) to provide opportunities for access to higher education for those from disadvantaged backgrounds.

> We see widening participation as a broad expression that covers many aspects of participation in HE, including fair access and social mobility. We continue to emphasise – but with renewed focus – that addressing widening participation relates to the whole 'life-cycle' of a student in HE. This covers pre-entry, through admission, study support and successful completion at undergraduate level, to progress on to further study or employment.[1]

Many respondents felt there should be greater diversity and representation of BME staff at senior levels, particularly in positions of power. One respondent at a 'new' (post-1992) university expressed this, saying:

> We have primarily Black and ethnic students, but we don't have the same representation in the staff body and whenever something comes up, I feel we [Black members of staff] are constantly being wheeled out to represent the university, to show that the university is really representative and takes equality seriously. But that could mean that it is being a tick box exercise and I am not convinced that there are enough – or indeed any – Black people who are in senior management roles who serve on the senate and other committees that make real decisions that affect what is going on in the university (Black, female senior lecturer).

Another participant commented on the widening participation agenda.

> We have been forthright in our response to the widening participation agenda at this university. Because we are a traditional university that does tend to attract the traditional student, we have tried to challenge this. But, whilst that is a policy the university is proud of and we are in one of the most diverse cities in the UK for some reason we still have very few BME academic staff and even students who come here. I am not sure why that is, it would be interesting to ask the students why they choose particular universities – is it because of who goes there, or is it because of the courses they want to pursue (Black, male senior lecturer).

Research has suggested that students from BME backgrounds are more likely to attend their local universities where there is a critical mass of like-minded students with whom they can identify (Bhopal, 2010). Many of the respondents in this study felt that universities should be making active attempts to encourage staff from BME backgrounds to be part of their organisations. Some suggested that universities should develop particular schemes that would encourage BME academics to make applications to work in research intensive universities. One respondent specifically said universities should be more active in this approach.

> They [universities] should be looking to develop a better understanding of different experiences that members of staff bring to the institution and find out the ways they may feel excluded and what contributes to the feeling of exclusion and marginalisation and what can be done differently. In discussion, you feel yours is the voice in the wilderness and that no one's listening to you (Black, female professor).

Whilst universities said they were actively trying to promote inclusive agendas (though respondents said there was little evidence of this in terms of

Inclusion, equality and social justice 141

the recruitment of BME staff), respondents felt that there was little in practice to demonstrate this.

> If you as a Black male – in my case – keep on going on about diversity and equality you have to be careful. On the one hand, you are not taken seriously because they think you are just banging the drum about race and they tolerate you saying that. But on the other hand, there is a feeling that it's just you who thinks like that – so it can be very challenging sometimes. You have to be able to strike a balance, it has to be taken seriously and you shouldn't be afraid to say that these issues are important (Black, male senior lecturer).

Another respondent suggested that he tried not to raise issues of diversity in his department, because he did not want to be labelled as the 'Black male who always has to bring race into everything'. Consequently, he stepped back from these issues. He also felt that some colleagues would 'hold this against you later on'.

> I try to back off about race in my department. I feel that there is an assumption that I would and should be mentioning race from my White colleagues – so I don't mention it. That is difficult, because in some instances I feel I should have mentioned it. The issue here is that if you mention race in relation to diversity you have to be careful because then you have to keep mentioning it. Sometimes to say what you think isn't that helpful because you are labelled either as a 'trouble maker' or you won't ever get that promotion that you want! (Black, male research assistant).

Equality policies

Many of the respondents spoke about the importance of equality policies in universities. However, they were doubtful of the effectiveness of such policies.

> People need to look within themselves and how they are powerful, how their race, gender, class and power impacts on other people. You have to start with the individual. It has to involve listening to the voices of those who are disempowered, hearing and then acting on it. It may be heard, but not taken on board. We have many policies in place here, but why are they there? Is it because the university thinks that they will get into trouble if they don't have them or is it because the university wants to make a difference to ensure that they are making sure that their employees are acting on their policies? (Asian, female senior lecturer).

Some respondents indicated that equality policies were used as a 'tick box' exercise.

142 *Inclusion, equality and social justice*

> Universities have to have these policies because they are considered to be at the forefront of all equality and diversity issues. But often these policies are like ticking boxes so that the university can say they have addressed issues of diversity. But we have to see how that translates from a practical point of view. For example what structures have been put in place for a department or a university to be making changes to be more diverse or to be more inclusive? That is the evidence that universities are making some contribution to the difference to being more inclusive (Asian, female professor).

Others thought that the policies were a form of rhetoric – and were rarely acted upon.

> The policies are important and we need them. But time and time again we are going over the same ground of thinking about diversity and how we can be more inclusive, but what has changed? There have been some in roads with policies and how behaviour is tolerated or not tolerated – but to me we are just talking and not acting. From this perspective then, those policies become rhetoric – so we are not really going to make any changes (Asian, female senior lecturer).

Whilst it was important to have policies in place for ensuring and adhering to legal requirements on diversity and equality, many respondents did not feel that the policies were enough to create and instigate real change – both in the structures of the academy and wider changes in society. Some respondents, however, felt that it was the academy that could be a driving force for creating real change.

> The academic world – because of the way it is – it is meant to be inclusive, could be a real driving force behind some of the changes we would need to make it more inclusive. But many institutions do not want to take that step or that leap forward – because they may be afraid of how they are seen. If we have major organisations making a difference – such as employing a Black vice chancellor, or two – then this may give other organisations the confidence to follow suit. But that would be a bold step – and it would show real change and I am not convinced that there are many universities who will take that step (Black, female professor).

Respondents felt that when real practical measures were taken to be inclusive of BME communities, there could be a move from rhetoric to reality and practice.

> They [universities] pay lip service to it [inclusion and diversity] in theory and it is rhetoric. They are keen to show it's representative in terms of having evidence. But in practice it is not. It should just be visible and

there should be no need for policies. But we are keen on having policies – you know – reports and policy speak, but on a practical level it's just not there. It's implemented on a strategic level, but you don't see it practically (Black, male professor).

Others felt universities should be more forthright in promoting diversity and equity.

> I think they [universities] should be more aggressive in promoting an anti-racist agenda. I think issues of race ought to be at the top of the department's kind of measure of success. There should be a solemn frank discussion of social cleavages surrounding race, gender and sexuality and so forth and this should be part of the department's intellectual identity. Departments should be judged on how they take issues of race forward and how race is addressed in the department and their work practices (Asian, male senior lecturer).

Whilst respondents were not convinced about the place of equality policies in universities, many were sceptical about how inclusion worked in practice. The following section explores this aspect.

Does inclusion work in practice?

Many of the respondents were sceptical about the concept of inclusion. On the one hand they felt it represented a positive way forward for a greater understanding of diversity and equity but on the other hand many suggested that there was no real understanding of how inclusion could work in practice, particularly in relation to the experiences of BME academics. A number of respondents felt that positive discrimination would be a way forward, but others disagreed with this idea. A Black female lecturer said,

> Inclusion must entail a degree of compensation for the lack of opportunities that people have faced in the past. Those that argue that positive discrimination would be harmful and undermine *equality* fail to see that for the most part, the most privileged sections of society have experienced positive discrimination for centuries. Under the guise of *equal* opportunities a minefield of inequalities persists (Asian, male senior lecturer).

Some respondents expressed an understanding that positive discrimination was something that was seen as *convenient* for some groups and worked for the advantage of some and not others. They referred to the notion that White groups have always been in positions of power and have had the advantages of positive discrimination in ways that BME groups have not. Furthermore, this took place under the umbrella of 'equal opportunities' – but these equal opportunities did not exist for *all* groups. A Black female professor openly advocated the use of positive discrimination, if it meant that there would be greater representation of those from BME backgrounds at *all* levels of the academy.

> The concept of positive discrimination is controversial. It has been used in the States for a very long time, and I believe it has worked over there. Here, we tend to frown upon it and I think there is greater opposition to it. I think it is one way forward. If you accept that racial discrimination is a process and that is going on, then positive discrimination should counter that. Perhaps we should have overt policies in universities which say we have to employ a certain number of people from BME backgrounds to be more inclusive. But then you have to be careful and it could create a backlash with some [White] colleagues thinking that we as Black people are getting favourable treatment and it may be seen that certain individuals are only employed because of their race and I think that would be dangerous.

Other respondents wanted inclusion to entail procedural and structural change.

> Inclusion is about changing the structures, so that people's attitudes can be changed to make a difference for all people. It's about being open, about sharing and communicating and making knowledge as democratic as possible, particularly from a university perspective (Asian, male senior lecturer).

An Asian female professor felt that structural changes were the only changes that could contribute to real inclusion in higher education.

> I guess one of the things inclusion means is not having to apologise for being different. Inclusion for me is also a processual thing because there is not one single measure of inclusion. Inclusion – or the nature of inclusion – changes as the requirements of inclusion develop. So what was satisfactorily inclusive a year ago may not be satisfactorily inclusive today. It means being sensitive to people's differences and changing institutions and mechanisms and procedures accordingly. Being open to change and not a priori precluding some kind of concerns because they come from an identity of difference.

Many respondents felt that inclusion was based on a process of constant change that took place over a period of time. It was a concept or idea that would have to be revisited as a process. But at the same time, it was also about being able to instigate change in ways which would make a difference and reflect the reality of inequalities in society. A Black female research assistant said,

> Universities should reflect the societies we live in – society is not all White is it? We should think about how we can make changes in the university to make them more inclusive. Of course inclusion is a very important thing and it must happen in universities. But it is not one of those things that can happen overnight, it has to be a process and sometimes these things can take years to make a real difference.

Many of the respondents were critical of how universities approached the concept of inclusion, but instead spoke about it as *exclusion*. A Black African senior lecturer said,

> At the official level of the university they want to promote equality of opportunity or certainly prevent inequality of opportunity, or prevent inequality of access based upon race or ethnicity, it would be very difficult in my mind, unless it was blatant – it would be very difficult in my mind to change a department with not executing that responsibility or administering that responsibility unless one had a great deal of support in the department. And if a Black or ethnic minority member is complaining about that in the first instance that suggests there is very little support in the department anyway.

An Asian male senior lecturer reflected on university culture that was not overtly expressed but existed in a hidden sense.

> I suppose something that we should think about is the canteen culture that exists in the academy where practices are reinforced or recreated not intentionally but through traditions of behaviour which people external to that kind of culture can't really know of until they enter it. I suspect that's the same with senior scholars and academics that run departments and institutions and it might be discernible in staff meetings and senior professorial meetings. It's the people that you and I don't have access to, and even if we did the behaviour would change. Perhaps you need to look at the telescope the other way round, through the eyes of White academics.

For others, inclusion was about specifically addressing the question of racism.

> We need to address the subject of racism. I think there's discrimination and that needs to be dealt with. I believe it's institutional racism. It's something that permeates universities – that's my sense (Black, female professor).

Many of the respondents working in UK universities mentioned the REF exercise on several occasions. On the one hand, they thought the REF was a positive process; particularly in relation to how it operated by assessing outputs. Respondents felt that the process would be fair and one which would 'neutralise ethnicity'. The idea of fairness and 'neutralising ethnicity' was based on assessments being judged against a list of criteria which were applied to all academics (regardless of their ethnic background). Some of the respondents suggested that this had the potential to remove any unfair treatment or discrimination against individuals because of their ethnic background, gender or their class. In essence, articles would be judged on merit.

> I know that the REF is always an important process the all universities have to go through. I have a Black colleague who tells me that he would not be a professor if it was not for the REF and as a young academic following him, I agree because the REF puts pressure on university management generally and therefore they need to appoint people who can publish, or have the potential to publish. Now that literally neutralises ethnicity, it just eliminates ethnicity. So it creates a level playing field which means that if you publish and perform, off you go. If you don't, you stay at the same level. It doesn't matter whether you are White or Black. So in that sense, the REF is critical (Black, female professor).

Others said that the specific criteria attributed to the REF indicated that an element of objectivity could be achieved.

> The REF has specific criteria which I assume has to be followed and because there is a panel – and not just one individual person – it has to be a fair process. It means that you are judged on your work and not by who you are. It would mean that articles should be based on their quality and not just because they were written by certain individuals (Black, male professor).

However, other respondents saw this as a negative aspect of the REF.

> The REF is *supposed* to be a fair process but I am not convinced that it is. There will be some authors who will be expected to have written good articles in certain outputs, but how do you know that is the case? There would be certain biases towards certain journals or certain individuals, even certain new universities. So I am not so sure how fair the REF process is going to be in all honesty. It could be the same as always, the new universities will be marginalised and the elite will not and will be expected to do well – even if they don't [original emphasis] (Asian, female senior lecturer).

Another negative aspect of the REF that respondents mentioned was the recognition that there would be some bias towards journals which were not recognised in the West. Many respondents were not convinced that articles published in Africa, the Indian sub-continent or East Asia would be given the same recognition as those published in the UK or North America.

> Most of the good journals are based in America and of course there are quite good ones here in the UK. I am publishing in journals in Africa and these journals are ranked relatively lowly. What I can say is, is that because there is a particular focus on Africa? Or does the focus on Africa impact on them negatively? Or is it that they get bad, weak articles published in them or both? (Black, male senior lecturer).

An Asian female lecturer pointed out,

> A lot of my work is international because I do some of my research in India so that means my work is often published in journals that are more relevant to India. But here, they are seen in a different way and are not respected as much as they are back home. This makes it difficult when the REF takes place because those same articles are not given the same prestige nor have the same advantages here. It can then become unfair.

Respondents also mentioned bias in how 'impact' may be measured in the REF.

> There is something in the REF called impact. It's all about how you take your work to the outside, rather than the inside of the university. So, if you know how to use your research and the impact that goes with it that is ok, but if for example you are coming here as a new person, a lecturer who is starting out, you have to take time to find out about the industry, or which policy is relevant and which governmental department is interested in your work. So you are automatically disadvantaged if you have come from overseas because you don't know which organisations are relevant and which are not (Black, female research assistant).

Respondents displayed contrasting views on the REF, some saw it as objective and 'neutralising ethnicity' and others saw it as subjective and biased towards UK journals and organisations.

Equal treatment and pay

The literature suggests there is an acknowledged pay gap in higher education (ECU, 2011). Several reports have outlined the differences in pay salaries and grade points between female and male academics at higher education institutions (Times Higher Education, 2012). The data suggests that female professors tend to be concentrated on lower pay grades and salary bands compared to male professors who are either at the same institutions or the same grades (UCU, 2012). Some respondents suggested that they felt that they had been put on lower pay grades and salaries compared to their White colleagues.

> The area that I am not sure about and I am not sure if I can attribute it to is race, ethnicity or gender . . . or just the circumstances of the timing that I got my job, I don't know. It's the pay level and the grade at which you are employed. The level at which other people have been employed since has been on a higher grade than me and I can't be sure what I would put that down to, but I do think and know that there are some discrepancies here. I sometimes think it could be because of my race, but I don't have concrete evidence for it (Black, male senior lecturer).

A Black male professor said,

> One clear way in which I know I was treated badly was that despite being the most qualified person in the department I was put on the lowest salary and I know that. A White, male colleague who had begun at the same time as me, but who was less qualified was put on the top scale. I didn't find this out until 2–3 years into the job, and that too only accidentally.

Many of the respondents working in universities in the UK outlined their perceptions of pay inequalities in higher education in comparison to their White colleagues. The remainder of the chapter will explore some of the responses from academics working in universities in the USA.

Inclusion and diversity in the USA

Research in the US suggests that people of colour experience significant disadvantages in university faculties; particularly in relation to obtaining full professorships (and tenure), pay, allocation of administrative responsibilities and their credibility in comparison to their White colleagues (Jackson, 2008). There is some data to suggest that there are significant differences between the experiences of women of colour and men of colour. Women of colour in different faculty have different experiences with students (sometimes negative) compared to men of colour, they are often asked to take on more administrative roles than their White female peers and are often paid less than them and less than men of colour. Research also suggests that their tenure rates are lower than White males and females (Jackson, 2008).

Respondents in the USA were sceptical about the concept of inclusion and how it worked in universities in the USA. Many suggested that universities were not proactive enough in their efforts to ensure inclusion was

Inclusion, equality and social justice 149

taking place or that they did not understand the concept of inclusion and what it meant in terms of people of colour and how they were represented in faculties.

> I do think institutions take inclusion seriously, but I do not think their ideas are complex enough. For instance, I don't think they understand it fully, nor do I think there's an adequate commitment to change the status quo. There has to be a real commitment to want change to happen if inclusion is going to happen, but I don't think that is the case. There has to be a real desire on the part of senior managers to want change and to want change to happen (Black, male professor).

Others felt that the notion of inclusion in universities did not translate into practical ideas.

> It's all surface talk. There's little being done to include and retain students and staff of colour at my institution. The institution does not take these things seriously, even though there are rules and regulations in place which suggest these issues have to be taken seriously and I'm not convinced that will happen (Black, male associate professor).

Some suggested that even when institutions made efforts to take these issues seriously, there was still a general lack of understanding about how inclusive measures could be put into practice.

> Diverse leadership is needed and inclusive decision making processes which involve key stakeholders and marginalised populations and proactive policies and programming. Universities should consider hiring faculty of colour in clusters and set up structures for supporting faculty if they have tenure track positions. For students, they should invest more in retention programming (Black, female assistant professor).

Many felt that inclusion should happen at all levels and all stages of the academic career for people of colour.

> Inclusivity must happen at all levels, in representation, in decision-making, in the culture of the institution and the climate as well as critiquing one's own privileges. Inclusion for me does not necessarily address issues of equality and diversity. In fact, I think individuals at my institution are very pro-inclusion at the expense of ignoring and minimising the deeply historical, political and cultural issues that pertain to the disenfranchisement of non-dominant groups. In other words, in attempting to include everyone to avoid any type of separate treatment of non-dominant groups, these approaches also ignore the particular

group specific issues that affect these groups. In essence institutions make these issues less visible in attempting to promote an inclusive environment (Black, female assistant professor).

There was an emphasis on institutions attempting to be inclusive but not losing sight of the real differences between individuals.

Inclusion suggests a deliberate, sustainable effort to include *all* students and faculty while simultaneously being responsive to the particular needs, backgrounds and histories of all student and faculty groups. But at the same time, this cannot involve differentiation [original emphasis] (Black, male associate professor).

Inclusion was a nebulous concept and one that many respondents were sceptical about. Many respondents were not convinced that inclusion could be achieved in universities but felt that it was such organisations that should be ensuring that inclusion was a goal that could be achieved. This chapter has examined how BME identities in the academy are understood in relation to inclusion, equity and social justice. It has explored how processes of inclusion and exclusion position BME academics in the White space of the academy.

Note

1 http://www.hefce.ac.uk/whatwedo/wp/policy/ [Accessed 16 May 2014].

References

Agocs, C. and Burr, C. (1996) Employment equity, affirmative action and managing diversity: Assessing the differences. *International Journal of Manpower.* 17 (4/5), pp.30–45.

Ainscow, M., Booth, T. and Dyson, A. (2006) *Improving Schools, Developing Inclusion.* London: Routledge.

Apple, M. (2013) *Can Education Change Society?* London and New York: Routledge.

Armstrong, A., Armstrong, D. and Spandagou, I. (2010) *Inclusive Education: International policy and practice.* London: Sage.

Banks, J. (1995) Multicultural education: Historical development, dimensions, and practice. In Banks, J. and McGee, C. (eds) *Handbook of Research on Multicultural Education.* New York: Simon & Schuster, pp.3–29.

Banks, J. (2007) *Educating Citizens in a Multicultural Society.* New York: Teachers College Press.

Barton, L. (1998) Markets, managerialism and inclusive education. In Clough, P. (ed) *Managing Inclusive Education: From policy to experience.* London: Paul Chapman, pp.78–90.

Bartz, D., Hillman, L., Lehrer, S. and Mayburgh, G. (1990) A model for managing workforce diversity. *Management Education and Development.* 21 (5), pp.321–326.

Bhopal, K. (2010) *Asian Women in Higher Education: Shared Communities.* Stoke on Trent: Trentham.

Bobo, L. and Hutchings, V. (1996) Perceptions of racial group competition: Extending Blumer's theory of group position to a multiracial social context. *American Sociological Review.* 61, pp.951–972.

Bonilla-Silva, E. and Forman, T. (2000) 'I am not a racist but . . .' Mapping White college students' racial ideology in the USA. *Discourse and Society.* 11 (1), pp.50–85.

Bowen, W., Chingos, M. and McPherson, M. (2009) *Crossing the Finish Line: Completing college at America's public universities.* Princeton, NJ: Princeton University Press.

Cochran-Smith, M. (1997) Knowledge, skills, and experiences for teaching culturally diverse learners: A perspective for practicing teachers. In Irvine, J. (ed) *Critical Knowledge for Diverse Learners and Teachers.* Washington: American Association of Colleges for Teacher Education, pp.27–87.

Deem, R. and Morley, L. (2006) Diversity in the academy? Staff and senior manager perceptions of equality policies in six contemporary UK higher education institutions. *Policy Futures.* 4 (2), pp.185–202.

Delgado, R. and Stefanic, S. (1992) Images of the outsider in American law and culture. *Cornell Law Review.* 77, pp.1258–1297.

Easley, C. (2001) Developing, valuing and managing diversity in the new millennium. *Organization Development Journal.* 19 (4), pp.38–50.

Edelman, L., Riggs Fuller, S. and Mara-Drita, I. (2001) Diversity rhetoric and the managerialisation of law. *American Journal of Sociology.* 106, pp.1589–1641.

Equality Challenge Unit (ECU) (2011) *The Experience of Black and Minority Ethnic Staff in Higher Education in England.* London: ECU.

Fulcher, G. (1989) *Disabling Policies? A comparative approach to education policy and disability.* London: Falmer.

Gill, P. (1996) Managing workforce diversity: A response to skill shortages. *Health Manpower Management.* 22 (6), pp.34–37.

Grant, C. (1994) Best practices in teacher preparation for urban schools: Lessons from the multicultural teacher education literature. *Action in Teacher Education.* 16 (3), pp.1–18.

Grant, C. and Sleeter, C. (2007) *Doing Multicultural Education for Achievement and Equity.* London and New York: Sage.

Jackson, J. F. L. (2008) Race segregation across the academic workforce: Exploring factors that may contribute to the disparate representation of African American men. *American Behavioral Scientist.* 51, pp.1004–1029.

Kalev, A., Dobbin, F. and Kelly, E. (2006) Best practices or best guesses? Assessing the efficacy of corporate affirmative action and diversity policies. *American Sociological Review.* 71, pp.589–617.

Kandola, R. and Fullerton, J. (1994) *Managing the Mosaic: Diversity in action.* London: Institute of Personnel Development.

Kidder, D., Lankau, M. and Chrobot-Mason, D. (2004) Backlash toward diversity initiatives: Examining the impact of diversity program justification, personal and group outcomes. *International Journal of Conflict Management.* 15, pp.77–102.

Ladson-Billings, G. (1992) Culturally relevant teaching: The key to making multicultural education work. In Grant, C. (ed) *Research and Multicultural Education.* London: Falmer Press, pp.106–121.

Ladson-Billings, G. (1995) Toward a theory of culturally relevant pedagogy. *American Educational Research Journal.* 32 (3), pp.465–491.

Ladson-Billings, G. and Tate, W. (1995) Towards a critical race theory of education. *Teachers College Record.* 97 (1), pp.47–68.

Leo, E. and Barton, L. (2006) Inclusion, diversity and leadership: Perspectives, possibilities and contradictions. *Educational Management Administration and Leadership.* 34 (2), pp.167–180.

Leonardo, Z. (2002) The souls of White folk: Critical pedagogy, whiteness studies, and globalization discourse. *Race Ethnicity and Education.* 5 (1), pp.29–50.

Lorde, A. (1992) Age, race, class and sex: Women redefining difference. In Andersen, M. and Hill Collins, P. (eds) *Race, Class and Gender: An anthropology.* Belmont, CA: Wadsworth, pp.495–502.

Marable, M. (1992) *Black America.* Westfield, NJ: Open Media.

McCombs, B. L. (2003). A framework for the redesign of K-12 education in the context of current educational reform. *Theory Into Practice,* 42(2), pp.93–101.

McDonald, M. (2005) *Doing Diversity: How teacher education programs in New York City intend to prepare teachers for diversity.* Paper presented to Annual American Educational Research Association Conference, Montreal, Canada, 13–15 April.

Montecinos, C. and Rios, F. (1999) Assessing preservice teachers' zones of concern and comfort with multicultural education. *Teacher Education Quarterly.* 26 (3), pp.73–93.

Nagda, B., Gurin, P. and Lopez, G. (2003) Transformative pedagogy for democracy and justice. *Race Ethnicity and Education.* 6 (2), pp.165–191.

Nieto, S. (2000) *Affirming Diversity.* New York: Longman.

Nieto, S. (2003) *What Keeps Teachers Going?* New York: Teachers College Press.

Ragins, B. (1995) Diversity, power, and mentorship in organizations: A cultural, structural, and behavioural perspective. In Chemers, M., Oskamp, S. and Costanzo, M. (eds) *Diversity in Organizations: New perspectives for a changing workplace.* Thousand Oaks, CA: Sage, pp.91–132.

Reskin, B. (2003) Including mechanisms in our models of ascriptive inequality. *American Sociological Review.* 42, pp.491–504.

Reskin, B. and McBrier, D. (2000) Why not ascription? Organisations' employment of male and female managers. *American Sociological Review.* 65, pp.210–233.

Rodriguez, N. (2000) Projects of whiteness in a critical pedagogy. In Rodriguez, N. and Villaverde, L. (eds) *Dismantling White Privilege: Pedagogy, politics, and whiteness.* New York: Peter Lang, pp.1–24.

Schultz, K. (2003) *Listening: A framework for teaching across differences.* New York: Teachers College Press.

Sleeter, C. (1996) *Multicultural Education as Social Activism.* Albany, NY: State University of New York Press.

Sleeter, C. (1993) How white teachers construct race. In McCarthy, C. and Crichlow, W. (eds) *Race, Identity and Representation in Education.* New York: Routledge, pp.157–171.

Sleeter, C. and Grant, C. (1987) An analysis of multicultural research in the United States. *Harvard Educational Review.* 57 (4), pp.421–445.

Sleeter, C. and Grant, C. (2003) *Making Choices for Multicultural Education: Five approaches to race, class, and gender.* New York: John Wiley & Sons.

Solomon, P., Potelli, J., Daniel, B. and Campbell, A. (2005) The discourse of denial: How White teacher candidates construct race, racism and White privilege. *Race, Ethnicity and Education.* 8 (2), pp.147–169.

Solórzano, D., Seja, M. and Yosso, T. (2000) Critical race theory, racial micro aggressions and campus climate: The experiences of African American college students. *Journal of Negro Education.* 69 (2), pp.60–73.

Strachan, G., Burgess, J. and Henderson, L. (2007) Equal employment opportunity legislation and policies: The Australian experience. *Equal Opportunities International.* 26 (6), pp.525–540.

Taylor P. (1995) Reverse discrimination and compensatory justice. In Cahn Steven, M. (ed) *The Affirmative Action Debate.* New York: Routledge, pp.9–14.

Thomas, D. (2001) The truth about mentoring minorities. *Harvard Business Review.* 74 (5) pp.99–105.

Times Higher Education (2012) We must see the gap to mind it. 2 August.

Tomaskovic-Devey, D., Zimmer, C., Stainback, K., Robinson, C., Taylor, T. and McTague, T. (2006) Documenting desegregation: Segregation in American workplaces by race, ethnicity, and sex, 1966–2003. *American Sociological Review.* 71, pp.565–588.

UNESCO (1994) *Salamanca Statement.* Paris: UNESCO.

UNESCO (2005) *Guidelines for Inclusion: Ensuring access to education for all.* Paris: UNESCO.

University and College Union (UCU) (2012) *The Position of Women and BME Staff in Professorial Roles in UK HEIs.* London: UCU.

Warnock, H. (1978) *Special Educational Needs: Report of the Committee of Enquiry into the Education of Handicapped Children and Young People* (The Warnock Report). London: HMSO.

Wilson, E. and Iles, P. (1999) Managing diversity: An employment and service delivery challenge. *International Journal of Public Sector Management.* 12 (1), pp.2–4.

Young, M. (1990) *Justice and the Politics of Difference.* Princeton, NJ: Princeton University Press.

Web references

http://www.hefce.ac.uk/whatwedo/wp/policy/ [Accessed 16 May 2014].

8 Conclusions

This book has attempted to explore the experiences of BME groups in higher education in two different social and economic contexts: the UK and the USA. By using empirical data from academics working in the UK and the USA, the book argues that whilst the social and economic climates in the UK are different, there are similarities in the experiences of those from BME backgrounds in higher education. Specific equality policies in the UK and the USA demonstrate the importance of policy legislation that is in place to remove or minimise disadvantages in the workplace so as to eliminate unlawful discrimination, harassment and victimisation. In the UK this has included the Race Relations (Amendment) Act 2000 and more recently the Equality Act 2010. The Equality Act includes advancing equality of opportunity between those who share 'protected characteristics' and fostering positive relations. It introduced 'protected characteristics' so that individuals could not be discriminated on grounds of their age, disability, gender reassignment, pregnancy, race, religion, sex or sexual orientation. In the UK the Equality Challenge Unit has developed the Athena SWAN Charter and at the time of writing is due to launch the Race Equality Charter. However, whilst there are significant policies in place in higher education, evidence suggests that the existence of such policies does not necessarily indicate that equality of opportunity has been achieved. Indeed research (Bhopal and Jackson, 2013; Bhopal, 2014) suggests that higher education institutions do not adequately address issues of racism, exclusion and discrimination. Furthermore, those in senior managerial positions view these aspects as tick box exercises particularly when addressing aspects of equality (Pilkington, 2013).

Similar patterns have been found in the USA; whilst there is a history of equality policy legislation such as *Brown v. Brown Board of Education*, 1954 and Title VII of the Civil Rights Act of 1964, there is evidence to suggest that racism continues to persist in higher education institutions, with those academics from Black African American backgrounds less likely to be concentrated in prestigious and research intensive universities compared to their White counterparts (Jackson, 2008). The USA has also seen an increase in the diversity of students attending universities, but this diversity is not reflected in the staff body (Jackson, 2008). Experiences of racism, discrimination and marginalisation are not particular to the UK and the USA; there is evidence to suggest that this is a world-wide phenomenon.

There has been a great deal of research exploring the experiences of academics working in the USA which points to lower salary levels for Black African Americans, heavier teaching loads, less time to spend on research and publications and lack of performance rewards compared to their White counterparts (Jackson, 2008). Similar findings have been reported in the UK with BME academics reporting feelings of isolation and a greater need for support and mentoring to advance their academic careers and promotion prospects (Bhopal and Jackson, 2013; Bhopal, 2014). The empirical data from this book reports similar findings, with BME academics reporting that they had less access to 'academic gatekeepers' compared to their White colleagues, which had a significant impact on their career progression and career trajectories. Respondents also reported feelings of being hired just because they were considered the 'token appointment', in order that faculties and departments were able to demonstrate their inclusivity.

Many of the respondents in the study were researching areas of race, diversity and inclusion related to aspects of social justice and many reported feeling disadvantaged because of this. Quite often, the research reported by Black academics was viewed as being 'personal research'. Some respondents who were working in research intensive universities where race was not seen as a high priority felt that a 'critical mass' would enhance the status of their work and its legitimacy. Many respondents also wanted to feel accepted in the academy, but continued to feel like 'outsiders'. The White space of the academy was one that was reserved for White colleagues who had a sense of entitlement and right to claim the space as theirs – something many of the Black academics reported that they did not possess. Other respondents (particularly women) spoke about their acceptance in the academy as being related to their 'presentation of self'. This was also linked to 'credibility' and acceptance in the academy.

Whilst many respondents reported experiencing racism, marginalisation and exclusion, they were keen to emphasise the importance of support networks and how they used them to overcome the negative aspects of their jobs. These support networks enabled them to gain emotional, academic and, for some, instrumental forms of support when they needed it. The support networks included formal and informal mentoring schemes, some of which were outside of their own universities. Support networks were also beneficial in providing access to networks which could influence and affect the careers of BME academics. Many suggested that compared to their White colleagues, Black academics were unlikely to have support networks which would enable them to have access to opportunities that would affect their careers. Hence, they worked together to ensure that they provided support for each other. These opportunities included being invited to present at keynote conferences, opportunities to join international networks and committees, to publish in specific outlets and to be on editorial boards. Despite the challenges many of the respondents faced, they were able to use successful strategies for support in the academy to ensure their success. For some this support came from their immediate and extended families as well as their local communities and churches. Religious networks were seen as being significant sources of support which were linked to a sense of community and belonging.

Many of the respondents spoke about how their White colleagues displayed a sense of privilege and entitlement towards certain aspects of their jobs. This was often highlighted when Black colleagues were successful in their roles. A significant number of respondents in the US spoke about the history of race relations and how this affected the positioning of Black people in US society, but also how they were positioned as Black academics in the White space of the academy. Whilst for many of the respondents being Black was based on a political identity, other identities such as class and gender were also important and often affected how individuals were positioned in the academy. Respondents were conscious of their own identities in the academy, particularly in relation to being a role model for their students and how this affected their careers. Respondents saw this as a positive aspect to their work, particularly when Black students looked up to them and thought that they too would be successful in the academy. Respondents from the UK emphasised this as an important aspect of their role and they worked hard to ensure that they were able to contribute to the positive experiences of BME students. Some respondents also spoke about how Black students actively wanted their support, over and beyond that of their White colleagues, and specifically wanted to work with them.

Many of the respondents who participated in the study spoke about the processes of promotion. Whilst there were specific criteria in place, there was a sense that subjective elements were also part of this process. Many of the respondents mentioned aspects of race, gender and class and the effect these had on the promotion process. For example for some of the respondents who were working in prestigious, research intensive universities indicated that class was a powerful and significant determinant of their position in the academy and that it was related to achieving promotion (particularly to senior levels such as full professor). Many of the respondents emphasised that they felt they had to work harder than their White colleagues to receive recognition for their efforts in their departments, and that there were different standards of work expected from them compared to their White colleagues. This was referred as a higher threshold of expectations from Black colleagues and evidence of a lack of trust in their work and the decisions that they made.

Respondents in the UK spoke about the REF which has created greater competition between universities, departments and faculties to achieve the best results and outputs from their employees. The REF itself has produced a greater segregation of teaching and research contracted staff, with an increased emphasis on competition between colleagues. Respondents in the UK had mixed feelings about the REF: some thought it was an objective exercise which worked to 'neutralise ethnicity' but others felt it was a far more subjective exercise which was biased in favour of individual REF panel members in relation to how particular articles and journals would be judged.

This book has argued that whilst academics in the UK and the USA are situated in two different social, economic and political climates BME academics working in universities in both the UK and the USA report similar experiences. Many BME academics in the UK and the USA continue to be positioned as 'outsiders' in the White space of the academy in which they have to negotiate their identities. If we are to move towards creating a society in which equity and inclusion are valued, change is required at all levels particularly in relation to inclusive policy making. As Apple states,

> it is possible to break away from a forged (and at times forced) consensus, thus opening up the space for a new social and educational imaginary . . . new educational structures are truly possible within the existing educational systems if social movements and political alliances are built that both challenge an accepted common sense and begin to create a new one.
>
> (2013: 127)

It is only then can we move towards greater equity, diversity and inclusion in higher education.

References

Apple, M. (2013) *Can Education Change Society?* London and New York: Routledge.

Bhopal, K. (2014) *The Experiences of BME Academics: Aspirations in the face of inequality.* London: Leadership Foundation for Higher Education, Stimulus Papers.

Bhopal, K. and Jackson, J. (2013) *The Experiences of Black and Minority Ethnic Academics: Multiple identities and career progression.* University of Southampton: EPSRC.

Jackson, J. F. L. (2008) Race segregation across the academic workforce: Factors that may contribute to the disparate representation of African American men. *American Behavioural Scientist.* 51, pp.1004–1029.

Pilkington, A. (2013) The interacting dynamics of institutional racism in higher education. *Race, Ethnicity and Education.* 16 (2), pp.225–245.

Index

A
academic gatekeepers 33
academy 70–4
Acker, S. 26, 37
Aday, L. 46, 58
Adeleye-Fayemi, B. 27, 37
Agocs, C. 130, 150
Ahmed, S. 21, 22, 37
Ainscow, M. 134, 150
Alger, J. 33, 37
Alldred, P. 55, 59
Apple, M. 3, 65, 135, 150, 157
Armstrong, A. 134, 150
Arvay, M. 57, 58
Athena SWAN 22–4, 154

B
Bailey, K. 49, 58
Banks, J. 136–7, 150
Banks, W. 37
Barton, L. 134, 150
Bartz, D. 13, 150
Bass, L. 68, 83
Bassanini, A. 37
Beattie, G. 7, 37
Beck, U. 6, 4
Behar, R. 57–8
Benini, A. 46, 58
Bennefield, R. 63, 83
Bensimon, E. 34, 37
Berg, B. 47, 58
Bergerson, A. 95, 111
Bertrand, M. 7, 37, 48, 58
Bhopal, K. 3, 4, 6, 10–12, 16, 24, 37, 52, 56, 58, 99, 100, 112, 140, 151, 154, 157

Black African American 31, 33
Black and minority ethnic (BME) academics 10; inclusion 12; students 17–19
Black Feminist research 56
Bonilla-Silva, E. 62, 83, 131–2, 151
Booth, C. 47, 58
Bourdeau, L. 48, 58
Brah, A. 56, 58, 99
Breakwell, G. 14–15, 37
Breuer, F. 57, 58
Brooks, J. 67–8, 85
Brown, D. 62, 83
Brown, N. 56, 58
brown on brown taboo 35
Brown vs Brown 27
Burke, M. 33
Burr, C. 130, 150

C
Carpenter, B. 61–2, 83
census 18
Cesare, S. 33, 37
Chapple, A. 46, 58
Charmaz, C. 50–53, 58
Chase, S. 54, 60
Chin, J. 65, 83
citizenship 137–8
Civil Rights Act 28
Clark, K. 18, 37
coalition government 9, 20
Cochran-Smith, M. 137, 151
coding 50–2
Collins, P. 27, 37, 56
colour-blind ideology 61–2
Corbin, J. 50, 60

credibility 124–9, 155
Crenshaw, K. 94, 98, 111
Creswell, J. 46, 55, 58
Critical Race Theory 26, 93–6, 138–9
Crofts, M. 10, 21, 38

D
data analysis 50
Davidson, A. 50–1; 58
Davis, D. 63, 84
Davison, K. 33
Dearing Report 12, 38
Deem, R. 10, 21, 38, 133, 151
De Laine M. 55, 58
De La Luz Reyes, M. 35, 38
Delgado, R. 94, 111, 138, 151
Diem, S. 61–2, 83
Diggs, G. 67, 83
Dillman, D. 47, 60
Dingus, J. 99, 111
Dingwall, R. 53, 60
discrimination, 8
diversity 21, 130–1, 133, 139–41; policy 22; USA 129
Dixson, A. 26, 38, 99
Dovidio, J. 7, 26, 33, 38
Drinkwater, S. 18, 37
Dujardin, A. 47, 58

E
Eagly, A. 65, 83
Easley, C. 133, 151
Eddy, J. 26, 39
Edelman, L. 130, 151
Education for All 133
Edwards, R. 55, 58
Elevations Trust Network 19, 38
entitlement 116–17
equality 26; USA 27
Equality Act 9, 20, 21, 154
Equality and Human Rights Commission (EHRC) 20
Equality Challenge Unit (ECU) 9, 16, 22–5, 38, 151, 154; consultation document 23
Equality Charter Marks 24–5, 38
equality duty 20
Equality Impact Assessments 21
equality policies 141–3, 154–5

Erickson, F. 33, 38
ethics 49, 50
Ezzy, D. 54, 59

F
Faircloth, S. 68, 83
feminist research 54–5
Feuerverger, G. 26, 37
Fontana, A. 47, 51, 59
Fredman, S. 10
Frey, J. 47, 51, 59
Fullerton, J. 131, 151
Further and Higher Education Act 12, 38
Futoran, G. 33

G
Gaertner, S. 7, 33, 38
gender 26–7, 31, 148; academy 65; BME 27; leadership 63; race 33;
Gender Equality Mark 23–4
George, A. 37
Gibson, S. 67, 83
Gill, P. 131, 151
Gillborn, D. 94–5, 111
Gillies, V. 55, 59
Glaser, B. 50, 59
Grant, C. 135–7, 151
Green, D. 10, 38
Gregory, S. 27, 38
grounded theory 50–2
Gunaratnam, Y. 56, 59
Guy-Sheftall, B. 94, 111
Gwele, N. 26, 31, 38

H
Habermas, J. 65, 84
Halcon, J. 35, 38
Hanrahan, K. 46, 60
Harding, S. 56, 59
Hartstock, N. 56, 59
Haskell, J. 56, 59
Heath, A. 7, 39
Henry, F. 27, 38
Henry, M. 55, 60
Hey, V. 10, 38
higher education 24; Black staff 31; Canada 26; Caribbean 27; power 35; South Africa 25; USA 29–30

160 Index

Higher Education Funding Council for England (HEFCE) 139
Higher Education Statistics Agency (HESA) 10, 13–18, 38
Hine, C. 47, 59

I

identity: Black 69, 104–5; gender, 54; positionality 52; in research process 52; subjectivity 55–6
Iles, P. 132, 153
inclusion 134–5, 143–50
intersectionality 79–80, 98–103, 156
interviewing 53

J

Jackson, J. 3, 6, 10–12, 37, 154, 157
Jackson, J. F. L. 28, 31, 33–5, 39, 63, 148, 151, 154–5, 157
Jawitz, J. 25, 39
Jay, M. 69, 111
Jayaratne, T. 54, 59
Jean-Marie, G. 61, 67, 83
Jennings, M. 99, 111
Johnson, P. 7, 37
Jones, V. 69, 84
Josselson, R. 57, 59

K

Kalev, A. 129, 151
Kandola, B. 7, 39, 131, 151
Kaplin, W. 28, 39
Kazmer, M. 47, 59
Kelly, N. 57, 60
Kidder, D. 130–1, 151

L

labour market 7; discrimination 28
Ladson-Billings, G. 93, 111, 136–7, 139, 151–2
Lather, P. 55, 59
Lauer, A. 39
Law, I. 8, 39
leadership 61, 80
Lee, B. 28, 39, 49, 56, 59
Le Franc, A. 7, 39
Leo, E. 134, 152
Leonardo, Z. 95–6, 111, 138, 152
Lester, J. 68, 84

Lewis, G. 56, 59
Lewis, K. 9, 10, 39
Li, Y. 7, 39
Lindley, J. 1, 2, 6
Litchman, M. 50, 56–7 59
Lloyd-Jones, B. 63–5, 84
Lofland, J. 51, 59
Lofland, L. 51, 59
Lorde, A. 138, 152
Lumby, J. 14, 39
Lymperopoulou, K. 18–19, 39
Lynn, M. 99, 111

M

Macbeth, D. 57, 59
Machin, S. 1, 2, 6
MacPherson Report 19
Mahoney, M. 95, 112
Marable, M. 138, 152
Marchant, G. 33, 39
Marcuse, H. 65, 84
Markham, A. 47, 59
Mauthner, M. 55, 58
McCall, L. 99, 112
McDonald, M. 136, 152
Mehra, B. 56, 59
mentoring 67, 77–9
Mertz, N. 65–7, 84
micro agressions 138
Millburn, A. 1, 6
Miller, J. 68, 84
Milner, H. 61–2, 84
Mitchell, N. 68, 84
mixed heritage 110
Modood, T. 8, 40
Montecinos, C. 137, 152
Morley, L. 22, 133, 151
Mullainathan, S. 7, 37
multiculturalism 135
Murphy, E. 53, 60
Myers, C. 33, 35, 41, 66

N

Nagda, B. 137, 152
Nash, J. 99, 112
National Centre for Education Studies 30
National Equality Panel 8, 39
network of knowns 66, 77

networks 115–17
Newman, I. 33, 39
Niemann, Y. 26, 39
Nieto, S. 96, 112, 137, 152

O

Office for Fair trading and Access (OFFA) 139
Office for Standards in Education (OFSTED) 20
Office of National Statistics (ONS) 12, 40
Okolo, R. 26, 39
O'Leary, J. 19
Olsen, D. 26, 31, 40
one drop rule 110
outsiders 91–3, 155

P

Pager, D. 7, 40
Parameshwaran, M. 18–19, 39
Patitu, C. 35, 41
pay gap 16–17
Pfeiffer, D. 49, 60
Phoenix, A. 56, 60, 99
Pilkington, A. 10, 21, 38, 40, 154, 157
Pillow, W. 57, 60
positive discrimination 144
Preston, J. 100, 112
Prewett-Livingston, A. 33, 40
promotion 113–15, 121–2, 156
Psenka, C. 33, 41
Pyett, P. 57, 60

R

race 117
Race Equality Charter Mark 24–5, 154
Race Relations (Amendment) Act 19, 40, 154
racetalk 131–2
racism: aversive 33; higher education 8, 86–91, 113–38; inequalities 8; leadership 62–3; symbolic 31; USA 31
Ragins, B. 130, 152
Rallis, S. 57, 60
recruitment 66
reflexivity 56–7
religious networks 81

Research Councils United Kingdom (RCUK) 12
Research Excellence Framework (REF) 3, 10, 145–7, 156–7
Reskin, B. 129–30, 152,
respondents: employment 44.; ethnicity, 45; gender 44; privacy, 50; USA 45
revolving door syndrome 34
Rheinharz, S. 54, 57, 60
Riggins, S. 31, 40
Rios, F. 137, 152
Rodriguez, N. 138, 152
role models 119–21
Rooth, D. 8, 40
Rossman, G. 57, 60
Roth, W. 57, 58
Rousseau, K. 26, 38
Ruebain, D. 8, 22, 40
Russell, G. 57, 60
Ryan, J. 62, 84

S

Salamanca statement 133
sampling 48
Sanchez, P. 64, 84
Sanchez-Hucles, J. 63–4, 84
Sanna, L. 33, 40
Sarantakos, S. 49, 60
Schaefer, D. 47, 60
Schofield, J. 62, 84
Schugurensky, D. 35, 41
Schulze, S. 26, 38, 40
Science Engineering Technology (SET) 22
Science, Technology, Engineering Medicine Maths (STEMM) 22–3
Scott, S. 55, 60
Senior, O. 27, 40
Shiner, M. 8, 40
Shultz, J. 33
Skype interviews 47
Simpson, L. 17–18, 40
Singh, G. 10
Singh, K. 26, 40
Sleeter, C. 95, 112, 135, 137, 151–2
Smith, D. 33, 34, 40
Snowden, G. 19, 40
social class 19, 108–9

social justice 133, 136
social mobility 1
Solomon, P. 138, 152
Solorzano, D. 94, 112, 138–9, 153
Son Hing, L. 8, 40
Sproull, N. 49, 60
Stefanic, S. 138, 151
Stephen Lawrence 19
Steward, R. 31, 40
Stewart, A. 54, 59
Stovall, D. 94, 112
Strachan, G. 130, 153
Strauss, A. 50, 59, 60
students in higher education, 17
Sturges, J. 46, 60
Sullivan, J. 47–8; 60
support networks 67, 74–7, 80, 155
Sutton Trust, 1, 6, 9, 41
Sweet, L. 46, 60
Swim, J. 33, 40

T
Tack, M. 35, 41
Talpade, M. 26, 41
Tang, T. 26, 41
Tate, W. 139, 152
Taylor, P. 130, 153
telephone interviews 46
Thapar-Bjorkert, S. 55, 60
Theoharis, G. 61, 85
Thomas, D. 131, 153
Tierney, W. 26
Times Higher Education 16, 41, 153
Tobias, M. 7, 41
tokenism 34
Tolich, M. 25, 41
Tomaskovic-Devey, D. 129, 153
Tooms, A. 66, 85
Torres, C. 35, 41
Trix, F. 33, 41

tuition fees 2, 3, 12–13
Turner, C. 33–5, 41, 66
typecasting 34
Tytherleigh, M. 14–15, 37

U
UNESCO 133, 153
universities 12; BME staff 13; Russell Group 12; staff 13; USA 28–9
University and College Union (UCU) 16, 21, 41, 153
US Department of Education 31, 41
Usher, R. 54, 60
Uzzi, B. 67, 85

V
Vandeyar, V. 31, 35, 41

W
Wane, N. 26–7, 41
Warnock Report 133–4, 153
Weber, E. 31, 35, 41
white allies 118–19
Whiteness 26–7, 69, 74, 96–8, 103, 122–4, 138, 155–6
widening participation 9, 140
Williams, B. 28, 41
Williams, S. 28, 41
Wilson, E. 132, 153
Wyer, R. 33

X
Xie, B. 47, 59

Y
Yosso, T. 26, 41, 94, 112
YouGov 9, 41
Young, M. 67, 85, 136, 153

Z
Zebrowitz, L. 33, 41

Made in the USA
Middletown, DE
17 August 2020